my revision notes

Pearson Edexcel GCSE (9–1)
BUSINESS

Andrew Hammond

HODDER
EDUCATION
AN HACHETTE UK COMPANY

Although every effort has been made to ensure that website addresses are correct at time of going to press, Hodder Education cannot be held responsible for the content of any website mentioned in this book. It is sometimes possible to find a relocated web page by typing in the address of the home page for a website in the URL window of your browser.

Hachette UK's policy is to use papers that are natural, renewable and recyclable products and made from wood grown in sustainable forests. The logging and manufacturing processes are expected to conform to the environmental regulations of the country of origin.

Orders: please contact Bookpoint Ltd, 130 Park Drive, Milton Park, Abingdon, Oxon OX14 4SE. Telephone: +44 (0)1235 827827. Fax: +44 (0)1235 400401. Email education@bookpoint.co.uk Lines are open from 9 a.m. to 5 p.m., Monday to Saturday, with a 24-hour message answering service. You can also order through our website: www.hoddereducation.co.uk

ISBN: 9781510433472

First published in 2018 by
Hodder Education,
An Hachette UK Company
Carmelite House
50 Victoria Embankment
London EC4Y 0DZ

www.hoddereducation.co.uk

Impression number   10 9 8 7 6 5 4 3 2 1

Year   2022 2021 2020 2019 2018

Cover photo © VLADGRIN/iStock/Getty Images
Illustrations by Integra Software Serv. Ltd.
Typeset in India by Integra Software Serv. Ltd.
Printed in Spain by Graphycems

A catalogue record for this title is available from the British Library.

Get the most from this book

Everyone has to decide his or her own revision strategy, but it is essential to review your work, learn it and test your understanding. These Revision Notes will help you to do that in a planned way, topic by topic. Use this book as the cornerstone of your revision and don't hesitate to write in it – personalise your notes and check your progress by ticking off each section as you revise.

Tick to track your progress

Use the revision planner on pages 4 and 5 to plan your revision, topic by topic. Tick each box when you have:
● revised and understood a topic
● tested yourself and practised the exam questions, then checked your answers at the back of the book.

You can also keep track of your revision by ticking off each topic heading in the book. You may find it helpful to add your own notes as you work through each topic.

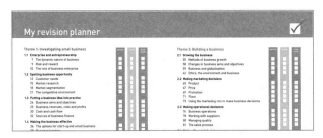

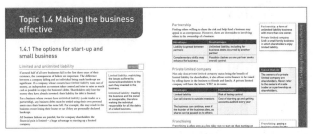

Features to help you succeed

Key terms

Clear, concise definitions of essential key terms are provided where they first appear.

Now test yourself

These short, knowledge-based questions provide the first step in testing your learning. Answers are at the back of the book.

Exam practice

Practice exam questions are provided for each topic. Use them to consolidate your revision and practise your exam skills. Answers are at the back of the book.

Exam tip

Expert tips are given to help you polish your exam technique in order to maximise your chances in the exam.

Typical mistake

The author identifies some typical mistakes candidates make and explains how you can avoid them.

Summary

A concise summary of all of the content covered in the chapter, to help you to see how all of the content fits together.

My revision planner

Theme 2: Building a business

REVISED   TESTED   EXAM READY

Countdown to my exams

6–8 weeks to go

- Start by looking at the specification — make sure you know exactly what material you need to revise and the style of the examination. Use the revision planner on pages 4 and 5 to familiarise yourself with the topics.
- Organise your notes, making sure you have covered everything on the specification. The revision planner will help you to group your notes into topics.
- Work out a realistic revision plan that will allow you time for relaxation. Set aside days and times for all the subjects that you need to study, and stick to your timetable.
- Set yourself sensible targets. Break your revision down into focused sessions of around 40 minutes, divided by breaks. These Revision Notes organise the basic facts into short, memorable sections to make revising easier.

REVISED ☐

2–6 weeks to go

- Read through the relevant sections of this book and refer to the exam tips, summaries, typical mistakes and key terms. Tick off the topics as you feel confident about them. Highlight those topics you find difficult and look at them again in detail.
- Test your understanding of each topic by working through the 'Now test yourself' questions in the book. Look up the answers at the back of the book.
- Make a note of any problem areas as you revise, and ask your teacher to go over these in class.
- Look at past papers. They are one of the best ways to revise and practise your exam skills. Write or prepare planned answers to the exam practice questions provided in this book. Check your answers at the back of the book.
- Try using different revision methods. For example, you can make notes using mind maps, spider diagrams or flash cards.
- Track your progress using the revision planner and give yourself a reward when you have achieved your target.

REVISED ☐

One week to go

- Try to fit in at least one more timed practice of an entire past paper and seek feedback from your teacher, comparing your work closely with the mark scheme.
- Check the revision planner to make sure you haven't missed out any topics. Brush up on any areas of difficulty by talking them over with a friend or getting help from your teacher.
- Attend any revision classes put on by your teacher. Remember, he or she is an expert at preparing people for examinations.

REVISED ☐

The day before the examination

- Flick through these Revision Notes for useful reminders – for example, the exam tips, summaries, typical mistakes and key terms.
- Check the time and place of your examination.
- Make sure you have everything you need — extra pens and pencils, tissues, a watch, bottled water, sweets.
- Allow some time to relax and have an early night to ensure you are fresh and alert for the examination.

REVISED ☐

My exams

Paper 1: Investigating small business

Date:...

Time: ....

Location: ....

Paper 2: Building a business

Date:...

Time: ....

Location: ....

Topic 1.1 Enterprise and entrepreneurship

1.1.1 The dynamic nature of business

Businesses change continually. They do this because the environment in which they operate changes. These changes mean that businesses need to adapt the products and services they sell if they are to remain successful. At the heart of continued success are new ideas.

Why new business ideas come about

REVISED

Changes in technology

Technological change enables the invention and production of new products. From the internet, through mobile phone technology to new materials used in sportswear, technological change allows businesses to launch new products. These products may well be more profitable for the business as they can charge higher prices for cutting-edge products. Technology also increases the chances of existing products becoming less popular, as they are more likely to become **obsolete**.

> **Obsolete**: a product or service with sales that have declined or come to an end as consumers find something new.

Changes in what consumers want

Fashions, tastes and personal habits change over time. As lifestyles change, with an increased desire for convenience in food products and an expectation that shopping can be done online, businesses must change what they sell or how they sell it. Fashion in clothing in particular can be very fast-moving, with the need for businesses operating in the fashion industry to introduce new products almost weekly.

Changes in what consumers want also present opportunities, particularly for those businesses that can react to these changes fastest. As demand for 'on-the-go' breakfast has risen, companies such as Mondelez have had huge success with their breakfast bars.

Products and services becoming obsolete

The result of these external changes is that demand for some products or services can disappear. Companies that can see their products moving towards becoming obsolete will be driven to come up with new products or services. Launching new products or services will enable them to maintain financial stability.

How new business ideas come about

In the dynamic world in which businesses operate, new ideas are vital. It is new ideas that allow a business to maintain their success as the world changes. New ideas can range from totally revolutionary concepts to minor adjustments to existing products.

Original ideas

The world is not short of original ideas. Most business students will have taken part in a lesson where they are asked to 'invent' a new product. Genuinely original ideas do not necessarily become successful products or services. Communicating the idea to others, actually being able to make the product (or figure out how to provide the new service) and then working out a successful way to market the idea to consumers are hurdles that prevent most original ideas generating successful products. For those that do succeed, however, the rewards can be great. Genuinely original ideas will, at least for a short time, face no competition. This allows them to corner their market and generate a return on the money spent developing the idea.

Adapting existing products/services/ideas

Most new products and services tend to be adaptations of existing ideas. Adaptations could include:

- new flavours
- different colours
- different pack sizes
- online access to a service
- faster ways to provide an existing service
- offering a way to personalise products for individual consumers.

Adaptations of existing successful products are more likely to succeed. The reason is that they are based on products or services that are already successful to some degree. There is a proven demand for that idea; the risk of failure is lower than for most original ideas.

Coming up with new ideas – both entirely original ideas and adaptations to existing ideas – is likely to be helped by:

- staff who are motivated and engaged in the work they do – for example, Google employees
- businesses choosing to spend a portion of any profit on new ideas instead of just paying out all of their profit to shareholders in dividends
- a diverse workforce, with different backgrounds generating a wider range of new ideas, more likely to reach a wider range of customers.

> **Exam tip**
>
> Notice how the sections on original ideas and adapting existing ideas offer a judgement on which is more likely to succeed. The judgement is justified by an explanation of why the risk of failure is lower. This process of 1) examining two contrasting issues, then 2) making a judgement that is justified, is at the heart of the exam skills you must demonstrate.

Now test yourself

1 List three reasons why businesses must continually consider changing what they do.
2 Identify one type of product that you own, where the rate of technological change is incredibly fast.
3 Why are adaptations to existing products more likely to be successful than original ideas?
4 How can a business try to ensure it is most effective in coming up with new ideas?

Answers on page 104

1.1.2 Risk and reward

Starting and running a business are risky activities. **Risk** centres on the uncertainty that things may go wrong, with negative consequences. Yet those willing to take risks will be those who stand to gain the **rewards** from owning a successful business.

Risk and reward: the balance between the worst that can happen and the best that can happen.

Risk

REVISED

Risk describes things that could go wrong. With such uncertainty involved in starting and running a business, risks are plentiful:

- Finding a large enough gap in the market
- Raising enough capital
- Getting the right people to work in the right way
- Building a customer base
- Retaining a customer base
- Running out of cash in quiet times
- Running out of energy and self-belief
- Coping with competition
- Growing too fast
- Coping with a growing workforce

Ultimately if one or more of these things go wrong, there are three fundamental consequences for entrepreneurs.

Business failure

Half of UK start-ups fail within five years of starting. This failure carries more than just financial consequences. An entrepreneur's reputation will be damaged, their esteem may take a major hit and the stresses caused by business failure create huge personal pressures for the entrepreneur and their family.

Financial loss

If a sole trader or partnership business fails, the owners are personally liable for any debts the business has built up. If any business fails, the owners may lose all the money they have invested in their business. For smaller businesses (sole traders and partnerships), the owners may lose personal assets that they are forced to sell to cover the debts their business has built up.

Lack of security

Giving up the safety of a paid job, working for a business where income is assured and predictable, leads to a lack of security. Most entrepreneurs endure tough times, where their income dries up and they may wonder where the money to pay the mortgage or feed and clothe the kids will come from. Losing the financial security that comes with being an employee, rather than an entrepreneur, is a major risk.

Exam tip

When exploring different types of ownership, you should be willing to link the type of liability (limited or unlimited – see 1.4.1) to the level of risk faced by business owners. Sole traders and partnerships, with unlimited liability for debt, face far greater personal financial risk.

Reward

REVISED

Business success

The sense of achievement that comes from starting and running a successful business is immense. Knowing the risks that have been overcome or avoided intensifies the sense of achievement felt by entrepreneurs. It often explains why some entrepreneurs are not content to simply start one business; they keep on starting new businesses, chasing the sense of triumph again and again.

Profit

Although some entrepreneurs will be content with making enough profit to live a comfortable lifestyle, others seek to become rich. Many will become rich by selling their business, either to a larger firm or to shareholders via the stock market. Either way, the rewards may run into the millions for some lucky and/or skilful entrepreneurs.

Independence

Some people really dislike being told what to do by others. Starting a business can represent a release from the need to follow instructions, or do it somebody else's way. An entrepreneur will have a significant level of independence over how they run their business and make decisions. For some, this independence is enough of a reward.

Now test yourself

TESTED ☐

1 State three risks involved in starting a business.
2 State three major rewards that entrepreneurs may receive if they successfully start their own business.
3 Why do all businesses face risks?

Answers on page 104

Answers on page 104

> **Exam tip**
>
> Note that in some situations, an entrepreneur may not experience the independence they might have wanted. Partnerships and limited companies with more than one owner will require agreement and compromise between the owners. Meanwhile, starting up as a franchisee often leaves entrepreneurs feeling frustrated about how strictly the franchisor controls how they are allowed to run the franchise.

1.1.3 The role of business enterprise

The role of business enterprise and the purpose of business activity

REVISED ☐

Deep-thinking business students may have asked themselves why businesses exist. The basic answer has three elements: to produce goods or services that people want to buy; to meet customer needs or wants; and to add value.

To produce goods and services

In order to live, we humans require certain basic goods, including food and shelter. These are usually produced or provided by businesses. Most people in the UK are also lucky enough to be able to afford to buy things that make our lives easier or more fun. These may be **goods**, such as mobile phones, or **services**, such as shopping centres or restaurants.

To meet customer needs

Businesses produce goods and services in order to meet **customers' needs and wants**. Selling products that meet our basic needs, such as food, drink and clothing, can be fairly straightforward as they are essential to customers. Selling products that meet customers' wants, such as a Netflix subscription or a VR headset, can be trickier, since consumers must be convinced that they want to buy this type of product in the first place, then to choose to buy from your business. The result is that firms that exist to fulfil customer wants may need to work harder on advertising, customer service and product or service design.

> **Goods**: physical items that may be fresh, such as apples, or manufactured, such as Heinz Baked Beans.
>
> **Services**: provide useful ways to help people live their lives – for example, shops, restaurants and hospitals.
>
> **Customer needs**: the products or services people need to make life comfortable.
>
> **Customer wants**: what people choose to spend their money on, once the weekly bills have been paid.

To add value

Businesses do more than simply pass on materials to consumers. They do things that increase the amount that people are willing to pay for the materials. In this way, successful businesses can cover the costs of providing products and make an extra amount on top: profit. The actual materials used to produce a can of Coca-Cola are likely to cost less than 5p. However, mixing those ingredients, packaging them in an attractively designed (and highly recognisable) can, and distributing that can to a convenient location for you to purchase it all add to the amount you are willing to pay. The business is **adding value**.

The main ways in which businesses add value are:

- **Convenience** – As consumers in the UK become wealthier, they will pay more to get things more easily and quickly. This may be by having food delivered or simply to save time preparing a meal by buying a supermarket ready meal.
- **Branding** – Adding a brand to a product or service may increase the price consumers are willing to pay. This may be because the brand carries an image they can identify with or want to be seen or associated with.
- **Quality** – A product that is manufactured to the very highest standards of quality can also increase the value consumers place on it; they know it will work perfectly and reliably and will therefore pay more.
- **Design** – If a business designs a great-looking product, consumers will pay more, simply because of the look of the product.
- **Unique selling points** – If a business is able to add a unique selling point to its product or service that consumers want, consumers have no choice but to pay the price charged, as that product will be the only way they can access the feature.

> **Value added**: the difference between the selling price and the cost of bought-in goods and services (the difference that creates the possibility of profit).
>
> **Branding**: giving a product or service 'personality' with a name and logo that makes it stand out.
>
> **Unique selling point (USP)**: an original feature of a product that rivals do not offer.

The role of entrepreneurship

REVISED

Entrepreneurs create and build businesses. Successful entrepreneurs must show a wide range of skills if they are to drive their business to success. The three main roles that an entrepreneur must fulfil are summarised below.

> **Entrepreneur**: a business person who sees opportunities and is willing to take risks in making them happen.

Organises business resources

Businesses use a range of resources, from materials and equipment to people, money and property. Ultimately an entrepreneur must be responsible for finding a source for these resources and arranging for them to arrive in the right place at the right time. They must also ensure that the resources work together to produce a product or service and that the process runs smoothly time after time, not just once.

Makes business decisions

Starting up and running a business means making decisions. Every day presents entrepreneurs with decisions to make, from choosing suppliers and selecting a new member of staff, to deciding how best to handle a delivery delay. Some of these may be major decisions that affect the whole future of the business, such as what to sell and where to sell it. The best entrepreneurs will get the big decisions right, and most of the smaller ones too. They will make the decisions rather than delay making a decision and they will effectively recognise the options open to them in any scenario.

Takes risks

Section 1.1.2 considered the main risks involved in starting a business. Entrepreneurs must be willing to accept and live with these risks. Without the willingness to take on risk in the hope of a reward, business start-ups simply would not happen.

Now test yourself

TESTED

1 State three ways that businesses try to add value.
2 List three types of resources that an entrepreneur must organise effectively in starting up a new restaurant.
3 State three key roles that businesses play in society.

Answers on page 104

Summary

New business ideas may come about as a result of:
● changes in technology
● changes in what customers want
● products becoming obsolete.

Sources of new business ideas may be either entirely original ideas or adjustments to existing products and services.

The three main risks faced by an entrepreneur are:
● business failure
● financial loss
● loss of security.

Three main rewards that entrepreneurs may enjoy are:
● business success
● profit
● independence.

The main roles of businesses in society are to:
● produce products and services
● meet customer needs
● add value.

The main ways in which businesses try to add value are:
● quality
● design
● USPs
● convenience
● branding.

The three key roles an entrepreneur must fulfil are:
● organising resources
● making business decisions
● taking risks.

Exam practice

1 Explain one method a manufacturer of lunch boxes could use to add value to their product. [3]
2 Explain one risk faced by an entrepreneur. [3]
3 Outline what is meant by 'the dynamic nature of business'. [2]
4 Discuss why new business ideas may come about. [6]
5 Discuss the rewards an entrepreneur may enjoy if they start a successful business. [6]

Answers on page 109

ONLINE

Topic 1.2 Spotting business opportunity

1.2.1 Customer needs

What are customer needs?

REVISED

Customers making the decision over which product to buy consider a range of factors. They will have various needs they expect a product or service to satisfy. Identifying and understanding these needs will help businesses to be successful. Usually, customers will look for a combination of the features identified below, though each customer will prioritise them differently.

Price

Most customers will consider the price of a product or service. At certain times, or for certain customers, lowest price may be their most important consideration. For those who are better off, or considering a special treat, price may be lower on the list of priorities. What is certain is that price will almost always be a consideration, so businesses must ensure the price is low enough to meet most customers' needs.

Quality

Although often seen as a clear trade-off with price, discount supermarkets such as Aldi and Lidl have shown that quality and low prices can go hand in hand. Quality may well be a key issue for consumers with higher income levels.

Choice

Most consumers value the chance to choose their favourite version of a product. Although too much choice can be overwhelming, some choice is often demanded by consumers where different flavours, colours or specifications are easily provided. Providing choice makes life harder for businesses, for whom making one standard product is easier and more efficient, but if consumers expect choice, it must be offered.

Convenience

Time is precious to customers and so they expect businesses to make the purchase of their products as convenient as possible. If a bank provides convenient ways to pay in money, or a vending machine provides a convenient place to buy a drink, consumers save time. The result is that they are willing to pay more for the convenience; in effect, they are paying to save time. This also explains the rise of 'ready meals', which speed up the process of preparing a meal, but cost significantly more than the individual ingredients.

Being efficient and reliable

A shop with unstocked shelves but with plenty of stock in the storeroom is being run inefficiently and, if customers cannot get the products easily, will be seen as unreliable. When buying products that are expected to last a long time, such as washing machines or other kitchen appliances, reliability may be an especially important factor for customers.

> **Typical mistake**
>
> Too often answers about consumer needs ignore price. Very few people are wealthy enough to ignore the price being charged. Other needs must be well met if price is to be successfully set above competitors'.

Providing great design

A further feature considered by many customers is design: how good a product looks. For many, the products they buy are part of the personal image they want to create. It is therefore important for firms to sell clothes that will make consumers look and feel great, to sell phones that look sophisticated or to sell cars that make consumers look successful or exciting.

The importance of identifying and understanding customers

REVISED

By identifying and understanding its customers' needs, a business is better able to produce the products they want, in the way they want them. This helps increase the sales of the business and so contributes to securing its long-term survival.

The keys to meeting customer needs are:
● genuinely understanding who your customers are and what they value
● having great product developers who can produce an item that gives customers the feeling they want.

As explained previously, consumers generally expect most of these needs to be met to a certain extent. The table below shows how a combination of needs creates certain expectations about different business situations.

Business situation	Key issues to consider when trying to meet customer needs
Café in a university student area	Cheap prices, with generous portions; open till late; free Wi-Fi; some reference to Fairtrade or organic produce
Dentist	Minimum wait; minimum pain; minimum nagging about a lack of flossing or too many sweets/sugary drinks
Buying a new family car	Friendly, efficient service; reliability; easy and fun to drive; good in-car entertainment; designed to feel spacious; good fuel efficiency
Manufacturing scarves	Great designs to meet different people's needs; different price levels: £6.99 scarves for teens, £19.99 scarves for middle-aged customers; making sure stock is available in all designs, especially in the autumn

Successful businesses must understand the needs of their customers. This understanding will come from effective market research and good instincts. These will allow the firm to judge which customer needs to prioritise with their different products. The challenge then becomes internal: being able to organise the resources available to the business in order to actually deliver what customers want.

Now test yourself

TESTED

1 List the six main customer needs.
2 Which two needs are likely to be most important for:
   a) Apple launching a new iPhone
   b) Ford launching a new small car aimed at first-time drivers
   c) an entrepreneur offering a nappy delivery and collection service?

Answers on page 104

Exam tip

An answer to a question about identifying customer needs will usually benefit from linking this to market research: the main mechanism a business has for finding out what consumers want. This will help you to build a chain of logic in your answer, linking business ideas.

1.2.2 Market research

In order to discover what customer needs are unfulfilled, **market research** is probably the answer. Even small-scale research, if well thought through, can provide great insights for entrepreneurs. Large businesses will spend many thousands of pounds on research to better help them understand needs of current and potential customers.

> **Market research**: the process of gathering, processing and interpreting information about consumers' behaviour.

The purpose of market research

REVISED

Carrying out market research fulfils several different but related purposes for a business.

To identify and understand customer needs

A successful business must understand what customers want, so finding out about their needs (and understanding which have priority) is a key purpose of market research.

To identify gaps in the market

If market research can identify customer needs, then research that picks out which needs are already being filled by other products may reveal un-met needs: a gap in the market. These represent excellent opportunities for businesses to exploit.

To reduce risk

The major risks involved in launching a new product are:
● The market may not want the new product.
● There may be demand for the product, but not enough to cover the costs of developing and launching the product.

Sensibly conducted research should identify whether either of these problems exists in advance, thus reducing the risk involved in launching a new product.

To inform business decisions

Decision makers always face a challenge as they are making a choice about an uncertain future outcome. Market research can help to reduce the uncertainties involved in the future prospects of a business choice, improving the quality of decision making.

Methods of market research

REVISED

We divide the methods of market research according to whether the data gathered is new or existing and what type of information we are trying to discover.

Secondary research

Using information that has already been gathered is usually the first step in the research process. The advantages and disadvantages of **secondary research** are listed below:

> **Secondary research**: when a company uses research that has already been carried out for general purposes.

Advantages
● Often free or available at low cost.
● Usually conducted on a large enough scale to be reliable.

Disadvantages

- Information may be out of date.
- Often fails to answers the specific questions that the business has.

Secondary research sources include:
- reports on whole markets from large market research companies such as Mintel and Key Note
- government statistical reports
- newspaper articles
- other internet-based sources.

Primary research

Primary research helps to answer the precise questions you need answers to. Although secondary data may help work out what questions to ask, it is primary research that will really reveal consumer needs specific to your business.

Advantages

- Provides up-to-date information.
- Focused specifically on a business's requirements.

Disadvantages

- Takes time to collect and analyse.
- Can be quite expensive to collect.

A range of methods is available to a business that is planning to conduct primary research.
- **Online survey** – These are a cheap, useful way to get basic feedback. They can be used regularly to check on whether customer attitudes are changing. They will, however, often only be answered by certain types of people, so may not provide reliably representative results.
- **Questionnaire** – Asking respondents a series of set questions, usually face to face, can provide reliable data on how customers will behave or what type of customers may be most interested in a product. However, conducting these on a large enough scale to provide reliable data may be time-consuming and expensive.
- **Focus group** – A small group discussion, led by a trained researcher, these can give firms real insights as to why customers do what they do, which can prompt new ways of doing things for a business. However, the cost per person interviewed will be very high.
- **Observation** – Watching, for example, the route a customer takes through a shop can offer clear information on problems with store layout. To spot patterns, however, may take a long time, increasing the cost of this method.
- **Social media feedback** – Information and feedback received via social media can be both quantitative (e.g. ratings out of five) and qualitative (e.g. comments made by happy and unhappy customers). Social media feedback has become an important alternative to formal primary market research.

> **Primary research**: research conducted first-hand; it is tailored to a company's specific needs – for example, a quantitative sales estimate for a brand new chocolate bar.

> **Typical mistake**
>
> Primary research does not have to be carried out by the business itself. Especially for large firms it is common to employ a specialist market research company to carry out research for you. What makes research primary is whether it is gathering brand new information for a business's own purposes.

> **Focus group**: a group discussion among people selected from the target market; it draws on psychology to provide qualitative insights into consumer attitudes.

Qualitative and quantitative research

If the goal of research is to get as close to reliable factual information as possible, **quantitative data** is needed. The nature of quantitative data is that it attempts to be representative of a large group of people's views. To conduct and collate research on this scale is only possible if closed questions with a limited range of answers are used. This data is commonly gathered by researchers using questionnaires face to face or over the phone, or perhaps even by questionnaires that are sent by post or online.

The limitation of quantitative research is that it rarely explains why customers behave the way they do. To really uncover insights on consumer behaviour, in-depth questioning is required to generate **qualitative data**, typically through the use of a focus group.

> **Quantitative data**: gathered when factual research takes place among a large enough sample of people to provide statistically reliable results – for example, a survey of 500 people aged 15–24 years.
>
> **Qualitative data**: gathered by in-depth research into the opinions and views of a small group of potential or actual customers; it can provide insight into why consumers buy what they buy.

The use of data in market research

REVISED

It can be easy to focus on the data-gathering aspect of market research. It is vital to remember that data must be interpreted and then used to draw useful and accurate conclusions. Skilled analysts are required in order to understand exactly what data means for a business and how that meaning can be used by a business to improve what it does.

A further complication can be gathering unreliable data. This is especially true in the case of quantitative information, which is designed to mimic facts about a whole market. If only a few people have taken part in the research, or if the research was biased to include a particular type of person, the data gathered may in fact not represent the bigger group sampled, leading to wrong conclusions being drawn from the research.

> **Exam tip**
>
> If possible, note how the research was carried out. Question whether the method of choosing which people to ask may cast doubt on how reliable the results are. Look out for entrepreneurs who ask their friends' opinions; friends tend to try to answer in an encouraging but perhaps not honest way, which can lead to unreliable data and interpretation of research.

Now test yourself

TESTED

1 State two methods of gathering quantitative research data.
2 Explain why focus groups are a relatively expensive form of research.
3 List four possible purposes of market research.

Answers on page 104

1.2.3 Market segmentation

A major use of market research is to find out more about the consumers that make up a market. Instead of trying to create and sell a product that suits all types of consumers, smaller groups of customers can be identified. These smaller groups will have similar needs. Each smaller group, or segment, can be treated differently. This means a business is more likely to match the specific needs of each group. This is more likely to lead to sales success.

Identifying market segments

REVISED

Market segmentation relies on splitting a huge group of consumers into smaller groups. The first question is therefore how to identify and split up a larger group. Businesses will search for a feature of consumers that causes differences in their needs. So, perhaps older consumers in a market have very different needs to younger ones. If this is the case, segmentation will be by age.

Some of the most common features used to **segment markets** are explained below.

> **Market segments**: subsets within a market that have been identified as a result of market segmentation.

Location

For some products, especially foods, tastes vary by region. An ideal snack for a 'Cockney' may be very different to a Glaswegian's perfect treat. The result is that catering to the specific needs of a particular region can allow a firm to sell a product that really suits the needs of a certain group of consumers.

Income

How much money consumers have to spend will affect what they can buy. As a result, consumers on lower incomes will focus on value for money when making buying decisions. Others with more money to spend may be looking for style, design or quality in a product.

Lifestyle

Whether it be hobbies and interests or personal values and preferences (such as being a vegetarian), lifestyle choices offer opportunities to identify smaller groups from larger markets. Sometimes, a business may obviously target a product at people with a particular hobby – for example, Sports Direct will produce products specifically for people who enjoy a game of darts. However, **lifestyle segmentation** can be subtler. People who exercise regularly may be more likely to purchase sugar free drinks. At the other extreme, individuals who spend over 20 hours a week watching television may be more likely to spend more on a sofa, or buy more popcorn, than the average person. Whatever lifestyle category is identified, opportunities exist to tailor a product to suit their preferences, so meeting their particular needs more closely.

> **Lifestyle segmentation**: grouping people by common characteristics in how they live, from their participation in sports and leisure to their views on the environment, taste in music or even passion for trains.

Age

Your needs from a product will rarely be the same as those of your grandparents. Different age groups tend to look for different things in a product. Elderly mobile phone users may be less interested in the Snapchat capability of a phone and more interested in a simple to use handset that allows them to make phone calls. The ability to produce a product suited to a particular age group again means their needs can be addressed more precisely. It is this fact that explains why many people will pay a higher price for a product aimed specifically at them.

Other demographic factors

There are plenty of other ways to split up a large market into smaller groups that share similar characteristics. A major issue may be whether a consumer has children or not. This could easily represent opportunities for businesses to create products targeted to suit the needs of adults with young children, which would differ to the needs of those with teenagers or the needs of those without kids. Other clear **demographic** characteristics include:

- gender – where the needs of males and females may be vastly different in many markets
- race – a factor that can be especially important in cosmetics, eating out or music
- religion – where huge differences may exist in consumers' needs for clothing, food or toys.

> **Demographics**: the study of the statistical differences that exist within a population, both now and in the future.

Ways in which a market may be segmented

Market mapping

REVISED

As part of the segmentation process, a business may draw up a **market map**. This means identifying and representing the main competitors in a market on a diagram, set out as a graph with two axes. The real skill is deciding what to measure on the axes. The best market mapping manages to identify the two most significant aspects of difference in consumers' needs. These will appear on the two axes. The mapping process is shown on the next page.

> **Market map**: a diagram that measures where existing brands sit on a two-factor grid – for example, young/old compared with high price/low price.

Identify the two key features in the market, usually using market research		Plot existing competitors according to how they meet those two key types of need, often using market research		Use the map to identify gaps in the market or areas where a particular business is too focused

The mapping process

The example below shows a market map for chocolate confectionery. The map suggests that the two key issues considered by consumers when buying chocolate are:

● Is it a 'light bite' or a 'filling snack'?
● Is it a luxury, bought only rarely, or an everyday purchase?

Useful conclusions that can be seen much more easily from drawing this map are:

● There seems to be room in the market for a filling, luxury product.
● Mars (the manufacturer of Snickers, Mars and Twix) is relying heavily on everyday, filling products – an area of the market where health concerns are leading to a decline in sales.

Choosing what to measure on the graph's axes is probably the critical skill. This will be determined by which factors can be best used to segment a market. Typical axes include:

● high price/low price
● for the young/for the old
● modern/traditional
● for men/for women.

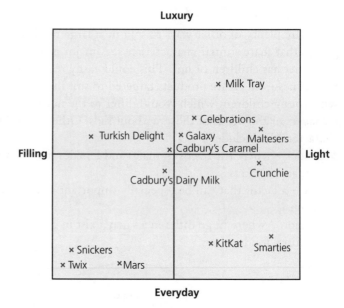

Chocolate market map (author's estimate)

Market mapping is undoubtedly useful in helping businesses to make decisions over which segments to target. However, market maps need careful consideration. A huge gap may exist because there is no effective demand for that product. Alternatively, a gap may exist because it is not possible for a business to fulfil two contrasting needs. A market map showing high price/low price plotted against high quality/low quality usually shows gaps for low quality but high priced products and for low price high quality products. This is because nobody wants to pay a high price for low quality products, while businesses may not be able to make a high quality product cheaply enough to charge a low price and still make a profit.

Now test yourself

TESTED

1 Explain why segmenting a market can help a business satisfy customer needs.
2 List four common methods of segmenting markets.
3 Explain why segmenting can allow a business to charge higher prices.
4 If you were drawing a market map for trainers, what would you put on the two axes?

Answers on page 104

1.2.4 The competitive environment

Most of the products and services we demand are provided by more than one business. In order for a business to survive, it must be able to persuade enough customers to use it, instead of the competition. A good understanding of their competitors will help a business succeed in the **competitive environment**.

> **Competitive environment**: the strength of competition between companies in the same market.

Strengths and weaknesses of competitors

REVISED

A useful way to understand the challenges offered by competitors is to research their strengths and weaknesses. Strengths may be features to avoid as a rival's unique product recipe, or brand name, may be unbeatable. Offering something that addresses a weakness in the competitors' products may be a good route to success.

Although managers or entrepreneurs may be able to assess competitors' strengths or weaknesses, a more accurate assessment may come from market research. A focus group discussing rival products may reveal great insights that a business can use to gain an edge over their rivals.

Key issues to examine about competitors include the following.

Price

How much do competitors charge and what do they offer for the price? Companies that charge higher prices for a better quality of service may have loyal customers who happily ignore cheaper prices because of the value they place on the extras offered.

> **Typical mistake**
>
> A student answer suggesting that a new, small business start-up can be successful by charging less than larger rivals lacks logic. Larger firms can usually negotiate better prices from their suppliers (reducing their costs) whereas a small firm, with higher costs, is unlikely to be able to charge a lower price than a larger firm and still make a profit.

Quality

Customers expect a certain level of quality. If companies make mistakes with quality, their rivals will soon steal their customers. A new business should invest a little of its money in buying products from rivals, so that they can identify those businesses for whom quality is a weakness. These are vulnerable to attack.

> **Typical mistake**
>
> Another mistake made by students is to suggest that the key to a successful business is to provide a higher quality product at lower prices than competitors. The problem here is that providing higher quality usually costs more. A business that has higher costs than its rivals is not likely to be able to cover those costs if their selling price is lower than competitors.

Location

Great locations for businesses can be a great help in gaining customers. This is especially true for firms selling products that are bought on impulse, for whom being in a busy place can be a key to success. However, great locations cost more. Higher rent for a great location places more pressure on the business to generate the sales needed to cover those costs.

Product range

A neat idea can be copied by competitors who can produce a slightly different product that does not break copyright or **patent** laws. This means that a competitor with a strong product, but only a limited range of variations, may have a weakness if a rival firm can produce something similar that meets a need.

> **Patent**: gives the inventor of a new product or process the right to be the only user; nobody can copy the idea.

Customer service

Giving customers what they expect when they buy is crucial. Failure to deliver on a promise, such as speed of delivery, or providing a service in an impolite or unhelpful way, suggests a customer service weakness. It is a weakness such as this that can allow another business to steal customers if they can deliver the right level of customer service reliably.

Impact of competition on business decision making

REVISED

The need to compete with rivals forces businesses to:
- offer good products and a good service
- keep prices down
- bring in new, **innovative** products or services to break away from fierce price competition.

These act to allow firms to maintain an edge over their competitors. If they don't, they will lose customers and sales to their rivals.

Competitors who begin to beat rivals may force managers at those rival firms to do things that they would prefer to avoid:
- cutting costs by cutting staff
- taking short-term action, such as cutting price, damaging the firm's reputation
- adopting **unethical** policies, such as dumping harmful waste in rivers.

> **Innovative**: a new, perhaps original, product or process.
>
> **Unethical**: an action or decision that is wrong from a moral standpoint.

Now test yourself

TESTED

1 What is usually the main problem with a great location?
2 Why is it useful to identify competitors' weaknesses?
3 Explain why cutting price to defeat a competitor may cause a long-term problem.

Answers on page 104

Summary

Customers have various needs, involving a combination of:
- price
- quality
- choice
- convenience
- great design
- efficiency and reliability.

Market research helps to:
- identify and understand customer needs
- identify gaps in the market
- reduce risk
- inform decision making.

Market research may be primary or secondary. Market research data may be quantitative or qualitative.
Market segmentation means splitting up consumers into groups with similar needs.

Markets may be segmented according to:
- location
- demographics
- lifestyle
- income
- age.

Market mapping is a useful tool in segmentation. The strengths and weaknesses of competitors can be identified based on:
- price
- quality
- location
- product range
- customer service.

Competition can force businesses to make choices they would prefer to avoid.

Exam practice

1 Which two of the following are methods of qualitative market research? (2)
   a) Observation
   b) Focus group
   c) One-to-one interviews
   d) Online surveys
   e) Postal questionnaires
2 Which method of segmentation is being used if consumers are divided up according to their gender? (1)
   a) Demographic
   b) Lifestyle
   c) Location
   d) Income
3 Which two of the following do competitors force businesses to do? (2)
   a) Follow legal obligations
   b) Offer a good price
   c) Develop innovative products
   d) Take a long-term approach to decision making
   e) Draw up a business plan
4 Which one of the following is not a common type of customer need? (1)
   a) Quality
   b) Price
   c) Convenience
   d) Promotion
   e) Great design
5 Explain one benefit to a business of using market mapping. (3)
6 Outline one benefit of using primary market research rather than secondary market research. (2)
7 Outline one benefit of using secondary market research rather than primary market research. (2)

Answers on page 109

ONLINE

Topic 1.3 Putting a business idea into practice

1.3.1 Business aims and objectives

A general sense of direction (the 'aim') and specific targets to aim for (the 'objectives') help organisations and individuals achieve what they set out to achieve. They do this by helping to ensure that everyone is pulling in the same direction, meaning decisions and actions are co-ordinated to effectively reach those targets. Often, businesses will try to ensure their objectives are:

- **S**pecific
- **M**easurable
- **A**chievable
- **R**ealistic
- **T**ime-bound

> **Aim**: a general statement of where you're heading – for example, 'to get to university'.
>
> **Objective**: a clear measurable goal, so success or failure is clear to see.

Aims and objectives for business start-ups

REVISED

Targets for start-ups are particularly important, since entrepreneurs, especially those lacking experience, need a clear understanding of whether their business is doing well or needs improvement.

Financial aims and objectives

- **Survival** – Bringing in enough cash to pay the bills is needed if the business is to stand a chance of trading in one, two or three years' time.
- **Profit** – If more money is earned than spent, profit can help the entrepreneur pay their personal bills, or even get richer.
- **Sales** – Generating sales without worrying initially about profit is an increasingly common trait, especially among online start-ups.
- **Market share** – With increased market share comes greater power in the market, over suppliers and customers.
- **Financial security** – Ensuring that the business has sufficient cash to cover any debts brings financial security for the firm and owner.

> **Market share**: the percentage of a market held by one company or brand.

Non-financial aims and objectives

- **Social objectives** – Some entrepreneurs start businesses with the main intention of improving society in some way, using business methods. Examples include Traidcraft, the Co-operative Bank and John Lewis.
- **Personal satisfaction** – Some entrepreneurs seek the sense of satisfaction that comes from creating a successful business, or that cannot be found working for somebody else.
- **Challenge** – Starting and running a successful business presents many challenges that can be irresistible to some people who are driven to succeed in many different walks of life.
- **Independence** – The chance to be your own boss can be a key goal for entrepreneurs, especially those who are tired of being told what to do, in a previous job or even from their time at school.
- **Control** – The chance to retain control of your own destiny can also be a driver for entrepreneurs; build a successful business and they will have control over their working lives.

Why aims and objectives differ between businesses

Owners differ; they start businesses for different reasons. While some will pursue profit and growth, seeking to use their business as a vehicle to get rich, others will have started the business for social reasons, leading to different business objectives.

Another reason for aims and objectives to differ are differing beliefs in the best way to build a successful business. For some, growing fast is the key to establishing a firm, whereas for others, a secure financial base from which to grow more slowly is key.

> ### Now test yourself
>
> TESTED
>
> 1 Briefly explain the benefit to a new entrepreneur of having clear objectives.
> 2 List five financial objectives for businesses.
> 3 List five non-financial objectives for businesses.
>
> **Answers on page 104**

1.3.2 Business revenues, costs and profits

Perhaps no concept is more fundamental in business than profit. Making sure that a business receives more money from sales than is spent running the business is a challenge for all businesses. Understanding the basic financial terms used in business is key to understanding business.

Revenue

REVISED

Revenue is calculated by multiplying the selling price of the product by the quantity sold. So, if a business sells 1,000 mugs for £5 each, their revenue is £5,000.

Revenue = quantity × price

> **Revenue**: the total value of sales made within a set time period, such as a month.

> **Typical mistake**
>
> Not all of the money a business receives is revenue, only money made from selling the products it sells. Money invested by the owners is not revenue; it is called capital.

Price

REVISED

Knowing the price a business charges sounds easy, but for some firms, predicting price can be tricky.
- For example, some businesses sell in markets where prices change frequently in the short-term. This will often be the case for agricultural products or raw materials, such as cotton or oil. This is because demand and supply can change rapidly due to external factors.
- If competition is direct and fierce, prices may need to be changed regularly to stay competitive.
- Launching a new product may involve unplanned price cuts if sales are not as good as expected.

Quantity (demand)

Knowing how many products are sold allows revenue to be calculated. Forecasting the quantity that will be sold is the main reason why forecasting revenue is difficult for many businesses. With so many external factors affecting the number of customers using all businesses, not to mention changes in the amount customers buy, revenue forecasting is a tricky challenge.

Costs

Running a business involves spending money. It can often be easy to overlook some of the costs involved. This is why forecasting costs effectively can be hard for any entrepreneur.

- **Variable costs**

    If a business sells twice as many products as last month, they can expect the cost of materials to double. Any cost that changes in line with quantity demanded is called a variable cost. Examples include:
    - raw materials – potatoes for making crisps or coffee beans for making coffee
    - bought-in components – spark plugs for cars or zips for jeans
    - energy used in the production process such as electricity to power machinery.

> **Variable costs**: costs that vary as output varies, such as raw materials.

Exam tip

Variable costs are usually stated as a figure for each unit made. To work out total variable costs, multiply the variable cost per unit by the number of units produced or sold. For example, if the variable costs of a phone handset are £100 and a company sells 20,000 in a week, the total variable costs for the week are
£100 × 20,000 = £2,000,000.

> **Fixed costs**: costs that don't vary just because output varies, such as rent.

- **Fixed costs**

    Some costs must be paid no matter how busy a company is. Even when a restaurant is empty, rent must be paid, waiters' wages must be paid and interest must be paid on loans. These are fixed costs and, as these costs cannot be shifted, they tend to dominate the worries of entrepreneurs.
- Total costs

    Adding fixed costs to variable costs for any level of output gives a figure for total costs. If revenue is higher, a profit is made. If total costs are higher than revenue, the firm is making a loss.

Typical mistake

Fixed costs can change – just not in relation to output. Defining them as costs that do not change is therefore wrong. Rent may change if the landlord charges more per month, while most workers expect an annual pay rise, meaning that their salary would change from one year to the next.

Interest

One fixed cost that may need some calculation is the cost of **interest** on any loans a business has taken. The cost of a loan is the interest that must be paid, expressed as a percentage of the money borrowed. So if a business has a debt of £5,000 owed to the bank at an interest rate of 10 per cent, they will pay £5,000 × 10/100 = £500 per year in interest.

> **Interest**: charges made by banks for the cash they have lent to a business – for example, 6 per cent per year.

Typical mistake

Although loans must be repaid, the money used to pay back the loan is not treated as a cost. The only cost involved in borrowing money is the interest.

Profit and loss

Once all costs have been predicted and revenue has been forecast, the business can calculate the **profit** they expect to make. This is done by deducting total costs from revenue. If total costs are higher than revenue, the business will be left with a negative figure; in other words, they will have made a loss.

> **Profit**: the difference between revenue and total costs. If the figure is negative the business is making a loss.

Check through the worked examples below.

> **Example: Profit**
>
> 1 A coffee shop has variable costs of 25p per cup and weekly fixed costs of £1,200. It sells each cup of coffee for £2.
>   a) What are its profits in a week when it sells 800 cups of coffee?
>
>   Profit = total revenue – total costs
>
>   Total revenue = 800 × £2.00 = £1,600
>
>   Total costs – (£0.25 × 800) + £1,200 = £1,400
>
>   Therefore, weekly profit is £1,600 – £1,400 = **£200**
>
>   b) What are its weekly profits if sales double to 1,600 cups of coffee?
>
>   Total revenue = 1,600 × £2.00 = £3,200
>
>   Total costs = (0.25 × 1,600) + £1,200 = £1,600
>
>   Therefore, weekly profit is now £3,200 – £1,600 = **£1,600**
>
> 2 ABC Ltd sells motorbikes. It buys the bikes for £2,000 and sells them for £3,000. It also has weekly fixed costs of £4,000. a the profit if six bikes are sold in a week.
>
>   Profit = total revenue – total costs
>
>   Total revenue = 6 × £3,000 = £18,000
>
>   Total costs = (£2,000 × 6) + £4,000 = £16,000
>
>   Therefore, weekly profit is £18,000 – £16,000 = **£2,000**

Break-even output

Before starting any business enterprise, whether a new business or launching a new product, it is crucial to work out whether the idea is likely to generate any profit. In order to do so, the enterprise must sell enough to cover the costs of the venture. An entrepreneur can work out the **break-even** point – the number of products that must be sold in order to cover costs – for a new enterprise.

> **Break-even**: the level of sales at which total costs are equal to total revenue. At this point the business is making neither a profit nor a loss.
>
> **Sales forecasts**: the business's predictions of how much they will sell in a future time period.

To calculate the break-even point, use the following formula:

$$\text{Break-even output} = \frac{\text{fixed costs}}{(\text{selling price} - \text{variable cost per unit})}$$

This figure can then be compared to **sales forecasts** to see if the business is likely to surpass this minimum level of sales needed to cover its costs.

Margin of safety

Another use of break-even is to allow the calculation of the firm's current **margin of safety**. Knowing how much they can afford sales to fall by before they start to make a loss can allow an entrepreneur to make a sensible assessment of how serious any problems they might face will be. To calculate the margin of safety, use the formula:

> **Margin of safety**: the amount by which demand can fall before the business starts making losses.

Margin of safety = current sales – break-even output

Break-even charts

A helpful way to see how much a firm needs to sell to break even is to represent the information on a graph. To do this, follow the five stages below.

- **Stage 1** Draw two axes

  Two axes are needed, showing quantity sold along the bottom of the graph and costs and revenues, measured in £s, on the vertical axis.

- **Stage 2** Draw a fixed costs line

  Firstly, add a horizontal line to the graph showing fixed costs. This will be flat as fixed costs do not change as the quantity made or sold increases.

- **Stage 3** Draw a total costs line

  Now add a line that shows total costs. This line shows fixed and variable costs added together. Calculate total costs at minimum and maximum output. At zero output total costs will be the same as fixed costs as no units are being sold, so variable costs will be zero. To calculate total costs at maximum output, multiply variable costs per unit by the number of units at maximum output, then add fixed costs to this figure.

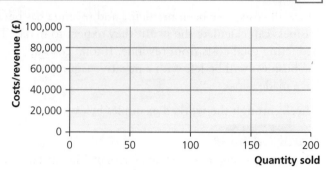

Stage 1 break-even chart

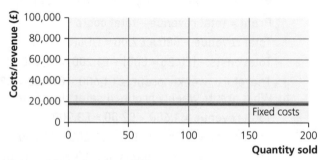

Stage 2 break-even chart

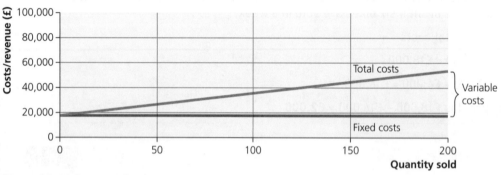

Stage 3 break-even chart

- **Stage 4** Draw a revenue line

  The next stage is to show the revenue made at all possible levels of sales. This means drawing a line to show revenue. Again, only two points need to be plotted and then a line drawn between them. Revenue when no products are sold will be zero, so the revenue line always starts at 0,0. Calculate revenue at maximum output by multiplying the number of units sold by the selling price.

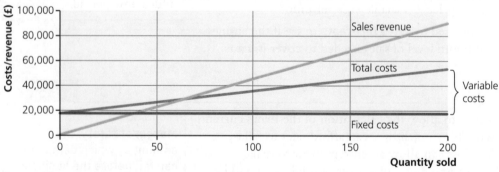

Stage 4 break-even chart

- **Stage 5** Read off the break-even point
  Find the spot where the revenue and total costs lines cross. By drawing a vertical line downwards to the axis showing quantity sold, the break-even output required to cover costs can simply be read off the axis.

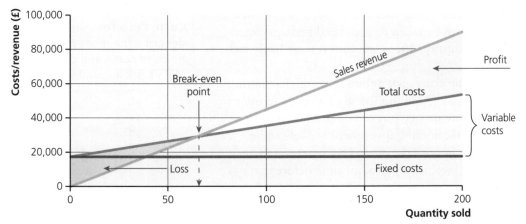

Stage 5 break-even chart

Now the power of the break-even chart is clear. By interpreting the break-even chart not only can we see the break-even point, but we can see the profit or loss made at any level of sales. This can be seen by measuring the vertical gap between the revenue and total costs line. The horizontal gap between current sales and the break-even point is the margin of safety.

The chart can also be used to show the effects of changes on the business. By drawing another revenue line, the effects of a change in price can be seen. Meanwhile, if costs change, a new total costs line can be drawn showing the effects of the change on break-even and profit.

The table below shows some of the crucial questions a break-even chart can help to answer.

Questions break-even can help answer	Impact on the break-even chart
Our landlord has increased our rent by 40 per cent. What will this do to our profitability?	Fixed costs line will rise, pushing the total cost line closer to the revenue line, i.e. cutting profits.
The recession has cut demand for our organic eggs by 20 per cent. What will be the impact?	No lines on the chart will change but the 20 per cent sales fall will reduce the margin of safety or perhaps wipe it out.
Is it right to cut our prices by 10 per cent? Will it increase or cut our profits?	The revenue line will rise less steeply, pushing it down towards total costs; profits can only rise if the sales volume leaps ahead.

Now test yourself

TESTED

1 Calculate the profit made by a business that sells 1,000 units for £10 each if its total costs are £8,000.
2 In the question above, what are the variable costs per unit if fixed costs are £5,000?
3 In the graphs used within this chapter, what are the:
   a) selling price
   b) fixed costs
   of the product being illustrated?

Answers on page 104

1.3.3 Cash and cash flow

Why does cash matter?

Cash matters because it is the only thing that can be used to pay bills. If bills go unpaid, the company can be taken to court and perhaps closed down. The two points in a company's life when cash is most likely to be problematic are:

- The start-up, because start-up costs such as building and decorating, staff recruitment and training and buying the stock needed to open up must all be covered before any money is received from customers.
- During times of rapid growth, because investment is likely to be needed to build bigger premises or take on and train extra staff, so costs will run at a higher level for a period of time before extra customers can be catered for and therefore bring in the higher levels of cash inflows needed to cover the higher costs.

> **Cash**: the term used to describe the money a firm holds in notes and coins and in its bank accounts.

The importance of cash to a business

The cash payments that businesses will need to make include:

- **Payments to suppliers** – This is for materials and services that the business needs to operate. Often, especially for established businesses, suppliers will offer 30 or 60 days' credit, so allowing the business time to find the cash to pay. However, if these bills are not paid on time, suppliers may stop supplying, forcing the business to stop operating.
- **Pay for employees** – Employees have a legal right to pay and depend on receiving their pay when it is promised in order to manage their own personal finances.
- **Overheads/bills that must be paid** – Rent and rates on premises and utility bills also need payment.

These payments may be especially hard to make if a large customer fails to pay on time. For example, a business may be expecting to receive £20,000 in their account from a customer on Thursday and have several large bills to pay on Friday. The £20,000 was enough to cover the bills; however, if the customer delays payment, the business may not have enough cash to pay wage or utility bills that are due.

Ultimately it is a lack of cash that forces all businesses to close against their will. If cash is not carefully managed, this means that the business will be unable to pay its bills, creating a situation called **insolvency**.

> **Insolvency**: when a business lacks the cash to pay its debts.

One additional thing to note is the difference between cash and profit. When a business sells an item to a customer and the item changes hands, a sale is made and revenue is generated. However, if the customer is given time to pay (given 'credit') – as is the case with many cars and sofas sold in the UK these days – the business selling the item will not immediately receive cash, even though they have generated revenue and therefore made a profit.

Selling on credit must therefore be carefully considered; a business needs to ensure that it will still have the cash needed to pay bills, or that customers will pay in time to ensure that bills can be paid when they become due.

How should cash be managed?

REVISED

Perhaps the most important tip for **cash flow** management is to ensure that careful cash flow forecasting is taking place. This is covered in detail a little later in this topic.

Other sensible cash flow management steps include:
- **Negotiate an overdraft** – This means that if a business needs a short-term supply of cash, the bank has already authorised this.
- **Keep costs under control** – This should help the business to remain profitable and a profitable business should never have serious cash flow problems. Keeping costs controlled helps to prevent cash draining out of the business.
- **Keep the cash coming in** – Given that so many business transactions take place on credit, it is vital to ensure that customers pay up when they are due to pay. Otherwise it is impossible to plan effectively for the future. If customers do pay on time, careful cash flow forecasting should help to manage cash effectively.

> **Cash flow**: the movement of money into and out of the firm's bank account.
>
> **Overdraft**: the amount of the agreed **overdraft facility** that the business uses.
>
> **Overdraft facility**: an agreed maximum level of overdraft.

Calculation and interpretation of cash flow forecasts

REVISED

Knowing when cash will be hard to find allows a business to take steps to prepare for these times in advance. This is why forecasting cash flows is perhaps the most fundamental step to successful cash flow management.

The actual **cash flow forecast** is a table that shows:
- bank balance at the start of each month
- cash inflows for the month
- cash outflows for the month
- the net cash flow for the month (inflows minus outflows)
- the bank balance at the end of the month.

The table below shows an example of cash flow forecast for a new nightclub.

> A **cash flow forecast** shows estimates of the likely flows of cash over the coming months and, therefore, the overall state of osane's bank balance.
>
> **Opening balance**: the amount of cash in the bank at the start of the month.
>
> **Net cash flow**: the figure showing 'cash in' minus 'cash out' over the course of a month.
>
> **Closing balance**: the amount of cash left in the bank at the end of the month.

Figures in 000s	Aug	Sept	Oct	Nov	Dec	Jan
Opening balance	250	65	−10	0	5	35
Cash inflows	0	0	85	65	115	55
Cash outflows	185	75	75	60	85	60
Net cash flow	−185	−75	10	5	30	−5
Closing balance	65	−10	0	5	35	30

Successful cash flow forecasting relies on:
- accurate prediction of monthly sales
- accurate prediction of when customers will pay for what they have bought
- careful allowance for operating costs and the timing of payments for these
- careful allowance for other flows of cash, both out of and into the business.

Negative cash flow

If cash outflows are higher than cash inflows (net cash flow is negative) cash flow problems may arise. For a business with a healthy bank balance, surviving a few months of negative cash flow shouldn't be a problem. However, if cash flow is negative for a longer period, or if the business has a low or negative balance, it will need to take action to improve cash flow or face insolvency.

To improve cash flow, the following methods can be useful.

- **Cut stock levels** – This will be by selling items but not replenishing them. This will convert stock into cash, without committing that cash back into the form of more stock. In other words, cash is freed up for other uses.
- **Increase credit taken from suppliers** – Asking suppliers to allow you longer to pay a bill gives more time for the cash needed to be generated by the business's sales activities.
- **Reduce credit to customers** – Although customers may be annoyed, reducing the length of time they are given to pay will help to bring cash into the business faster.

Now test yourself

1 At what two points in a firm's existence is cash most likely to be a problem?
2 List four features of good cash flow management.
3 If a business starts the month with £200 in the bank, receives £600 of cash in, sees £700 of cash outflows, what will be their net cash flow for the month and their closing balance?

Answers on page 105

1.3.4 Sources of business finance

Businesses need money. Some will be used to buy things that the business will keep and use in the long-term and some will be needed to finance the day-to-day running of the business, such as paying bills and buying stock. The sources of this money should match the purpose of raising the money, ensuring that the finance is secure, not too expensive and offers the chance to get enough money to satisfy the need.

Long-term finance may be used to:

- start up the business
- finance the purchase of assets with a long life, such as property and buildings
- provide the money needed for expansion – for example, to build a bigger factory or buy another business.

Short-term finance may be used to:

- get through periods when cash flow is poor
- bridge gaps when large customers delay payment
- provide the extra cash needed to produce a sudden rush order from an important customer.

Sources of long-term finance

Personal savings

For many small businesses, the owners' savings are a major source of finance. Other potential investors want to be convinced that the owner is willing to plough their own money into the business before supporting the owner financially.

Share capital

Selling a share of the ownership of the business means the new shareholder receives part of the business. In return they pay for the shares they buy, which raises finance for the business. The shareholder receives one vote per share when the company's shareholders meet to agree on big issues and is entitled to a share of any annual profits that the business has made and decided to pay out as **dividends**.

> **Share capital**: raising finance by selling part-ownership of the business. Shareholders have the right to question the directors and receive part of the annual profits.
>
> **Dividends**: payments made to shareholders from the company's yearly profits. The directors of the company decide how much to pay out in dividends; in a bad year they can decide to pay out nothing.

Benefits	Drawbacks
The capital paid stays in the business. If the shareholder wants to cash in their investment, they will need to find somebody else willing to buy the shares.	If many shares are issued or sold, the original founders of the business may find their ownership is diluted. The key to maintaining control is to ensure you retain at least 50 per cent of the shares.
If the business does badly, no dividends have to be paid. Contrast this with the interest on a loan, which must be paid no matter how well the business has done.	If a business is listed on the Stock Exchange it can be taken over. This can affect business decision making, encouraging a focus on short-term profit rather than stable long-term growth.

Loans

A loan is usually obtained from a bank. Loans have three key features:
1 Interest payments must be made on time, otherwise the business may be taken to court.
2 Loans are usually secured against a business asset, so if the loan cannot be repaid, the bank can take the asset as a way of recovering their money.
3 Interest rates may be fixed or variable. Fixed rate loans provide greater certainty when planning cash flows, but variable rates may be lower.

> **Typical mistake**
>
> Interest payments are treated as a fixed cost for the business; they do not change in relation to sales. This is true even if the interest rate is variable; payments may change, but not in relation to sales.

Venture capital

Venture capital is offered as a mix of share and loan capital. The providers are willing to back fairly risky business ventures, more so than high street banks. However, in return they will expect a significant shareholding in the business, but will also provide part of the finance as a loan to secure interest payments.

> **Venture capital**: a combination of share capital and loan capital, provided by an investor willing to take a chance on a small- to medium-sized business.

Retained profit

The safest source of finance is profits made in previous years that are kept within the business and used to buy new assets. This is also the most common source of finance.

Crowdfunding

A more recent form of business finance, **crowdfunding** allows small, individual investors to put relatively small sums of money into new business ventures that may be too risky for banks or venture capitalists to consider.

Retained profit: profit kept within the business (not paid out as dividends); this is the best source of finance for expansion.

Crowdfunding: raising capital online through many small investors, though not through the stock market.

Advantages	Disadvantages
Acts as a mixture of financing method and market research; if the crowdfunding cannot attract enough investors, maybe the business idea is not going to work.	Often unsuitable for less exciting but feasible business ideas that don't attract small investors.
Offers the chance for entrepreneurs with no capital of their own to start up.	Most attempts to crowdfund do not reach their target level of investment.

Sources of short-term finance

REVISED

If finance is only needed for a short period, probably to deal with a cash flow problem that will sort itself out within a few weeks or months, short-term sources of finance are more appropriate.

Bank overdraft

This involves an arrangement with the bank to allow a business to keep spending even when their bank balance drops below zero. A limit is agreed and the firm can keep spending up to that level. The amount they actually use will vary from day to day; indeed, they may spend much of the time without using their overdraft if their bank balance stays positive. Key features include:
- a variable interest rate
- flexibility – interest is only paid on the amount used when it is being used
- the bank can demand repayment within 24 hours.

Trade credit

If suppliers offer the opportunity to buy now and pay later, this represents a source of finance for a business. Most suppliers offer credit to established firms, but new business start-ups often find it impossible to gain credit from their suppliers, who cannot be sure whether the business will keep trading long enough to pay for the goods supplied.

Trade credit is given when a supplier provides goods but is willing to wait to be paid – for perhaps up to three months. This helps with cash flow.

Now test yourself

TESTED

1 State the two common sources of short-term finance.
2 State three reasons why a firm may wish to raise long-term finance.
3 List two ways in which a bank loan causes cash outflows.

Answers on page 105

Summary

Business aims and objectives provide a general sense of direction and specific targets to aim for, which help organisations and individuals achieve success. They help to ensure that everyone is pulling in the same direction.

Financial aims and objectives include survival, profit, sales, market share and financial security.

Non-financial aims and objectives include social objectives, personal satisfaction, challenge, independence and control.

Aims and objectives differ between businesses due to different motives for starting businesses and different beliefs in how a business should be run.

Profit = revenue – costs.

Costs can be fixed or variable.

Break-even occurs when a business makes neither profit nor loss.

Break-even diagrams can show a business's financial situation as an aid to decision making.

To calculate a firm's break-even point, divide fixed costs by selling price minus variable cost per unit.

In business, cash is needed to prevent insolvency and to pay suppliers, employees and overheads.

A cash flow forecast shows opening balance, cash inflows, cash outflows, net cash flow and closing balance month by month.

Forecasting future cash flows is the key to successful cash flow management.

Cash and profit are different, mainly due to the use of credit by businesses when buying and selling.

Long-term sources of finance for business include personal savings, share capital, loans, venture capital, retained profit and crowdfunding.

Short-term sources of finance include bank overdrafts and trade credit.

Exam practice

The following information is available for Heath's Bioscience Ltd:

Selling price = £80

Variable cost per unit = £30

Fixed costs = £40,000 per month

Maximum possible output = 2,000 per month

Current sales = 1,800 per month

The company wants to expand capacity and is planning to buy new machinery that will cost £500,000. The effects of this are shown in the cash flow forecast below that covers the next six months:

All figures in £000s	Month 1	Month 2	Month 3	Month 4	Month 5	Month 6
Receipts/cash inflows	120	140	140	180	240	250
Payments/cash outflows	A	100	600	120	160	150
Net cash flow	20	40	(460)	60	80	100
Opening balance	60	80	120	(340)	(280)	(200)
Closing balance	80	120	B	(280)	(200)	(100)

The company must decide whether to use a bank loan or an overdraft to finance the purchase of the new machinery.

1 a) Calculate the current monthly profit made by the business. (2)
   b) Calculate the current break-even point for the business. (2)
   c) Calculate the current margin of safety for the business. (2)
2 Complete the two missing figures on the cash flow forecast, shown as A and B. (2)
3 Justify a decision on whether the business should use a bank loan or an overdraft to buy the new machine. (9)

Answers on page 110

ONLINE

Topic 1.4 Making the business effective

1.4.1 The options for start-up and small business

Limited and unlimited liability

REVISED

If around half of all new businesses fail in the first three years of their existence, the consequences of failure are important. The difference between a company failing and an individual being made bankrupt are significant. If a company whose owners have **limited liability** runs out of money, an independent accountant takes control and tries to raise as much cash as possible to repay the business's debts. Shareholders only lose the money they have already invested: their liability for debt is limited.

For a business whose owners have **unlimited liability** (a sole trader or a partnership), any business debts must be settled using their own personal assets once their business has none left. For example, this may result in the business owner losing their house or car if they are personally declared bankrupt.

All business failures are painful, but for company shareholders the financial pain is limited – a huge advantage to starting up a limited company.

> **Limited liability**: restricting the losses suffered by owners/shareholders to the sum they invested in the business.
>
> **Unlimited liability**: treating the business and the owner as inseparable, therefore making the individual responsible for all the debts of a failed business.

Types of business ownership

REVISED

In legal terms, different types of business ownership exist. The three most common are listed below, along with advantages and disadvantages of each. When an entrepreneur sets up a business, they will choose what type of business to start (most commonly a **sole trader**), by considering how the advantages and disadvantages meet their personal situation.

> **Sole trader**: a business run by one person; that person has unlimited liability for any business debts.

Sole trader

A sole trader is a business with a single owner – responsible for everything – making all the decisions and carrying all the risk. However, any rewards will also be all theirs and there is no paperwork involved other than telling the 'taxman'.

> **Typical mistake**
>
> Sole traders are the sole owners of a business, but can employ staff to work for them.

Advantages	Disadvantages
Can start trading immediately	Unlimited liability
Have 100 per cent control	Have 100 per cent responsibility for the business, making holidays and illness a problem

> **Exam tip**
>
> Sole trader status suits simple, small businesses that are unlikely to run up any major debts. The owner keeps control and has no major formalities other than paying their tax.

Partnership

Finding others willing to share the risk and help fund a business may appeal to an entrepreneur. However, there are downsides to involving others in the ownership of a business.

Advantages	Disadvantages
Liability is spread between partners	Unlimited liability, including for business debts incurred by another partner
Complementary skills may enhance the business	Possible clashes as one partner seeks overall control

Private limited company

Not only does **private limited company** status bring the benefit of limited liability for shareholders, it also allows extra finance to be raised by selling shares in the business to friends and family. A private limited company will have the letters 'LTD' in its name.

Advantages	Disadvantages
Limited liability	Risk of losing control
Can sell shares to outside investors	Cost of starting up and getting accounts audited every year
The business can continue, even if the founder of the business dies, as shares can be passed on to others	

Typical mistake

The owners of a private limited company are shareholders. Never refer to the owners of a sole trader or a partnership as shareholders.

Franchising

Franchising is often seen as a less risky way to start up than starting an independent business from scratch. Buying a franchise in an existing business can certainly bring advantages. However, for an entrepreneur, taking this option will not be cheap and may bring frustrations.

Advantages	Disadvantages
The franchisee receives the right to use a recognisable name and logo, as well as a tried and tested method of running a business.	Royalty payments must be made to the franchisor, usually a percentage of revenue, perhaps as much as 8 per cent.
As franchisees will pay into a central fund for advertising, the franchise can be advertised nationally, perhaps on TV.	In addition, the initial fee to buy a franchise can be expensive.
With a tried and tested method, franchises have a lower failure rate than independent start-ups, meaning banks are more willing to lend to franchisees.	If the franchisor fails the franchisees will be dragged down.
	If other franchises are poorly run, their bad reputation may negatively impact custom at your franchise.

Now test yourself

TESTED

1 Why is limited liability important for a business that will buy most of its supplies on credit?
2 Which two types of business have unlimited liability?
3 Why may the owner of a franchise make less profit than the owner of a successful independent start-up?

Answers on page 105

1.4.2 Business location

Choosing the right place to locate a business can be the most important factor affecting success. Four main features of a location are likely to affect most location decisions.

Factors influencing business location

Proximity to the market

The market is the customers a business is hoping to sell to. Being near to where customers live, work or travel makes it easier and more convenient for those customers to visit the business. This means that **proximity** to market will be crucial for a business providing a service that customers must be there in person to receive, such as a hotel or a gym.

> **Proximity**: nearness to, so proximity to materials means how near a location is to the materials required by the business.

Proximity to labour

With most businesses needing staff to work for them, if employees cannot be found, the business faces problems. Some firms will need specially skilled staff or perhaps enough staff willing to work at minimum wage level. Although a certain amount of travelling can be expected for staff, there are limits to how far staff can practically travel to get to work, making this an important factor.

Proximity to materials

Although all businesses need supplies of some kind, some are more reliant on having a reliable supply of materials. Those that use bulky materials to produce a relatively small product will find transport costs reduced if they locate closer to materials than to their market.

Proximity to competitors

Instinct suggests, correctly for many businesses, that avoiding competition is a positive feature of a location. Being the only business of its type in a local area means customers unwilling to travel have little choice. However, for some types of business, locating close to competitors makes sense. Restaurants and bars do better if they are located in city centres, where most people go out for the evening: avoiding competitors may mean avoiding customers.

Nature of the business activity

As has already been suggested, the right location for some businesses is the wrong one for others. If a business faces a location decision, the most important issues will involve the nature of the business itself. The table at the top of the next page shows the types of business that will be most concerned about each of the major location factors.

> **Exam tip**
>
> Many exam questions will explore which location factors are more important to different businesses. Context is key, as explained in this section on the nature of business activity.

Some businesses will need to take into account one or more location factors when deciding what the most important issues are. An example of such a business might be a car assembly plant, where proximity to materials and availability of skilled labour will both be crucial.

Location factor	Type of business
Proximity to customers	Where customers have to visit to consume the product or service, e.g. hairdressing salon, nail bar, pub, restaurant
Proximity to materials	Where supplies are bulky and huge quantities are needed
Proximity to labour	Where skilled labour is needed and perhaps this is concentrated in only a few areas
Proximity to competitors	Locate close to competitors when customers visit a certain area for a certain purpose, such as city centres for nights out (bars, restaurants) or in out-of-town shopping centres (many retailers). Locate away from competitors where it is hard to make your business stand out from other rivals (dry cleaners, convenience stores).

Impact of the internet on location

Internet-only businesses, such as clothing firm ASOS or eBay, would be less concerned about the 'traditional' location factors. For these e-commerce businesses, keeping costs low may be more important, enabling them to charge the lower prices we expect online. The table below shows a comparison between the location issues faced by the online company ASOS and the high street fixed premises retailer Primark.

	E-commerce business, such as ASOS	High street retail business, such as Primark
Head office location	Can be anywhere	Can be anywhere
Product display	On a single website, allowing heavy investment in quality photos and customer interaction	In-store, so carrying high property and staff costs in multiple locations (and with too few design experts)
Stock range	Can keep every size and colour in stock, so customer disappointments should be rare	Space constraints in many store locations may mean restricted choice of colours and sizes
Customer services location	Can be anywhere; having a single location keeps costs down	In-store, therefore carrying high property and staff costs in multiple locations
Delivery to customer	Critical to have efficient deliveries; may be hard in crowded cities	Not a problem

Making a location decision

With most business decisions, making the right choice depends on a balance between revenues and costs. The same is true for location decisions. While a more expensive location, with a higher rent, may present problems covering costs, the reason it is expensive is likely to be that it provides better access to customers. As a result, more expensive locations are likely to bring in higher revenues. Therefore, an entrepreneur needs to carefully consider whether the higher revenues promised by a more expensive location will outweigh the higher costs (rent, staff wages, business rates) incurred by the better location.

Now test yourself

1 State the four major location factors.
2 Which factor is likely to be most important for a new café?
3 Why do Primark locate in busy high streets?

Answers on page 105

1.4.3 The marketing mix

The marketing mix is made up of the four major issues that a business must decide on when marketing its product or service. All four factors begin with a P and so are sometimes called the 4Ps. Taken together, they create the overall image that consumers will decide to buy or not to buy.

The 4Ps

REVISED

Product

Decisions about what **product** or products to sell are the heart of the mix. However, aspects of the product, such as how it is designed, what functions it fulfils and what different variations are made available, can set the tone for the rest of the mix.

Price

Although a high **price** bringing a higher profit from every unit may be tempting, it is only likely to be the right choice for firms selling exclusive, high quality products. Other businesses will choose to set a low price – aiming to be cheaper than any rivals – while others will set an average price, using other elements of the mix to help them stand out.

Promotion

This is called **promotion** because the activities in this section of the mix are all active attempts to promote increased sales of a product. These may be designed to have a long-term effect, advertising on television or in cinemas, or a short-term impact, using sales promotions such as buy one get one free deals.

Place

Choosing where and how to distribute the product (**place**) is vital in ensuring that consumers can get it when they want it. Different types of products may be distributed in different ways, from snacks through vending machines, shoes through high street stores or websites or digital music downloads through digital stores such as iTunes.

How the elements of the marketing mix work together

REVISED

To be effective, the 4Ps must complement one another; in other words, they must give off a clear message about the image the company is trying to create for its product. A low price for a high quality item sold through exclusive retailers will just give rise to suspicions from consumers about its real value.

> **Product**, as a part of the marketing mix, means targeting customers with a product that has the right blend of functional and aesthetic benefits without being too expensive to produce.
>
> Within the marketing mix this involves setting the **price** that retailers must pay, which in turn affects the consumer price.
>
> Within the 4Ps **promotion** means all the methods that a business uses to persuade consumers to buy – for example, branding, packaging and advertising to boost long-term image of the product and short-term offers.
>
> **Place** as part of the marketing mix means how and where the supplier is going to get the product or service to the consumer. It includes selling products to retailers and getting the products displayed in prominent positions.

Balancing the marketing mix based on the competitive environment

For most firms, the actions of their competitors may make it necessary to adjust their marketing mix. The goal must always be to stand out from rivals in some way. Therefore, if a rival company changes their product, new features may need to be added to make the firm's product stand out again, or a price cut by a rival may need to be matched. The real challenge is to find a way to ensure that the marketing mix is planned and does not simply react to rivals.

The impact of changing consumer needs on the marketing mix

As discussed in section 1.2.1, meeting consumers' needs is vital if a business is to succeed. As consumers' needs change, the elements of the marketing mix may need to be altered to ensure that the business continues to meet the changed needs of consumers. The table below shows three ways in which consumer needs have changed and the effects these have had on the marketing mix of many firms.

Change	Effect on marketing mix
Cycling changing from a leisure activity to getting to work daily/commuting	Distribution (place) changes from bike shops in the suburbs to bike shops in city centres
The boom in UK holidaymakers going to Thailand and South East Asia	Product development, such as Branston launching its Sweet Chilli Pickle in early 2016
Increasing consumer demand for 'free-from' foods, such as lactose-free and gluten-free	Despite food prices falling generally in 2015, 'free-from' food prices increased as suppliers took advantage of the surrounding hype

The impact of technology on the marketing mix

Major advances in technology can affect any element of the marketing mix. Although much of this will be the result of internet-based technologies, many other types of technology can affect firms' marketing mixes. The table below shows two examples.

Changing technology	Effect on marketing mix
The rise of m-commerce (mobile commerce): e-commerce on-the-go via apps rather than websites	Promotional offers have to be simpler and clearer so that they can be understood quickly
Hi-tech but lighter materials have made airplanes much more fuel-efficient and less polluting than in the past	There's an opportunity for flight prices to be cut, especially on long-haul flights
Digital communication, notably the use of email, text messaging or messaging apps	This can allow a business to send personalised promotional messages and offers directly to customers who have provided their details

Now test yourself

TESTED

1 List all four elements of the marketing mix.
2 What is the marketing mix trying to create for any company?
3 State three reasons why any successful business's marketing mix needs to change over time.

Answers on page 105

1.4.4 Business plans

The role and importance of a business plan

REVISED

The major function of the **business plan** is to enable outside investors to gain a clear understanding of the business that has approached them seeking finance. However, the plan should also be a vital document for internal use, by the entrepreneur. The process of drawing up the plan forces careful thought by the entrepreneur – always useful. Meanwhile, laying out the details of how the business will be run should enable the entrepreneur to be absolutely clear on how the business will have a competitive advantage over its rivals.

> **Business plan**: a detailed document setting out the marketing and financial thinking behind a proposed new business.

A business plan should have the following sections:

1 **The business idea** – This is a summary of what the business will offer from a customer perspective.
2 **Business aims and objectives** – Investors want to know what the business is aiming to achieve and whether that suits their purposes.
3 **Target market** – This will give a clear idea of what type of customers the business is aiming at, supported by market research.
4 **Marketing plan** – This will provide a broad overview of the approach the firm will take to marketing.
5 **Forecast revenue, costs and profit** – These allow a plan to show the break-even point and margin of safety.
6 **Cash flow forecast** – The importance of forecasting for cash flow management is especially acute at the time of start-up.
7 **Sources of finance** – With a cash flow forecast in place, the amount of finance required and the nature of the finance can be devised.
8 **Location** – Actually sorting out the right location will be critical to the business's success. Investors will expect to see details of the arrangements made.
9 **Marketing mix** – It is here that a detailed plan for the 4Ps can be outlined to show how the marketing plan will be enacted.

Exam tip

Always try to find the source of information included in a business plan. If the owner lacks experience, their own estimates may be highly unreliable and undermine the validity of information included in a plan.

The business plan: benefits and problems

Business plans should not be regarded as statements of perfect fact. They rely on estimates and research; however, careful research and estimates can offer reliable data to be included as the basis of forecasting for the business.

> **Typical mistake**
>
> Do not believe that providers of finance are naive. An entrepreneur whose forecasts are unrealistic will be found out when venture capitalists or banks look at their plan.

Benefits	Problems
Forces the entrepreneur to think carefully about every aspect of the start-up, which should increase the chances of success.	Making a forecast (e.g. of sales) doesn't make it happen; entrepreneurs sometimes confuse the plan with reality; poor sales can come as a terrible shock.
It may make the entrepreneur realise that she or he lacks the skills needed for part of the plan and therefore try harder to employ an expert or buy in advice.	Problems arise if the plan is too rigid; it is better to make it flexible, so that you are prepared for what to do if sales are poor (or unexpectedly high).
If the plan is well received by investors, they may compete to offer attractive terms for obtaining capital.	Plans based on high sales will include lots of staff to meet the demand; risks are lower if the business starts with a low-cost/low-sales expectation.
Many entrepreneurs have the whole plan in their head, not on paper; if illness or accident strikes, others will only be able to keep things going with a paper plan.	Business success is often about people, not paper. An over-focus on a perfect plan may mean too little time is spent visiting suppliers or talking to shoppers.

The purpose of planning business activity

Not only does business planning help entrepreneurs to spot potential problems before they occur, it is also critical to raising finance for the business. Although things will rarely go to plan, the process of putting the plan together should help to ensure that the entrepreneur not only has the best chance of gaining the finance they need, but has thought through possible problems and how they might deal with them. In essence, the role of a business plan is twofold: to help obtain finance and to help minimise risk.

Now test yourself

1 What is the main reason that entrepreneurs construct business plans?
2 State four of the nine sections that should be included in a business plan.
3 State two problems of writing a business plan.

Answers on page 105

Summary

The owners of a sole trader or a partnership have unlimited liability for business debts.

The owners/shareholders of a limited company have limited liability for business debts.

Entrepreneurs may choose to start up as a franchisee.

The major issues to be considered when choosing a location for a business are:
- proximity to market
- proximity to supplies
- proximity to competitors
- proximity to labour.

The most important factors will depend on the nature of the business.

Choosing the right location will involve balancing potential revenues with the costs involved in the location.

The marketing mix consists of:
- product
- price
- place
- promotion.

A successful mix must consist of four elements complementing one another to create a clear image.

The marketing mix may need to change as a result of:
- competitors' actions
- changing consumer needs
- technological change.

A business plan helps to raise finance.

A business plan should include:
- the business idea
- aims and objectives
- target market
- marketing plan
- forecast revenue, costs and profit
- cash flow forecast
- sources of finance
- location
- marketing mix.

Exam practice

Sophie Reid is planning to open a new high-class hair and beauty salon. Her experience working at a branch of Toni and Guy in the city centre has convinced her that there is a market for another high-class hairdresser in her city. She has some savings (£2,500), but knows she will need to raise an extra £17,500 to start up and is therefore producing a business plan to show to potential investors. She is planning to form a private limited company.

Sophie's biggest decision is where to locate the business. She has narrowed the choice down to two locations. The table below shows details of the two options.

	Location A City centre	Location B Outskirts of the city
Annual rent	£120,000	£26,000
Annual rates	£12,000	£8,000
Distance to nearest competitor	0.2 miles	3 miles
Average hourly footfall (people walking past per hour)	3,000	150

1 Identify two features of a private limited company. (2)
2 Outline two benefits to Sophie of producing a business plan before she starts her business. (4)
3 Which location should Sophie choose? Justify your answer. (9)

Answers on page 110

ONLINE

Topic 1.5 Understanding external influences on business

1.5.1 Business stakeholders

Businesses affect the lives of many. Not just employees and customers, but suppliers, local communities and even the government.

Stakeholders and their different objectives

Each group of **stakeholders** is likely to hope for slightly different things from the business.

The table below shows the major stakeholder groups and what each would like from a business, stated as the objective of the stakeholder group.

> **Stakeholders**: all those groups with an interest in the success or failure of a business.

Stakeholder	Different objectives of each stakeholder group
Shareholders (owners)	Shareholders in family-run, private limited companies usually focus on long-term organic growth. Shareholders in public limited companies (plcs) are more likely to care mainly about the short-term share price; they may be delighted to sell at a big profit if the company is bought by a rival, or to see sharp cost-cutting to boost profits
Employees	Security of employment; opportunities for career development (so organic growth is a key objective); fair pay and good 'fringe benefits' such as pensions, holidays and perhaps a company car
Customers	Consistently high quality products and service; honest and fair dealing from the company; bright, innovative new products that make life better (or more fun)
Managers	Security of employment; opportunities for career development (so organic growth is a key objective); fair pay and good 'fringe benefits' such as pensions, holidays and perhaps a company car
Suppliers	Honest and fair dealing from the company, especially on prices and credit terms; good communication about future plans; strong organic growth meaning rising demand for supplies
Local community	Honest and fair dealing from the company, especially on plans that affect local employment and the environment; some locals may want to see the business grow, others may not
Pressure groups	Honest and fair dealing from the company, especially on plans that affect customers and the environment; often pressure groups seem to be against growth, perhaps focusing overly on the downside of business activity
The government	Honest and fair dealing from the company, especially on tax arrangements, employment plans and location plans (HSBC threatened to leave the UK to try to water down legislation controlling banking practices; it succeeded)

> **Typical mistake**
>
> All shareholders are stakeholders, but not all stakeholders are shareholders. Remember that the shareholders are the owners of the business, so they will be affected by the business. However, other stakeholder groups, who are clearly affected by what a business does, do not own the business. Never use the words shareholder and stakeholder interchangeably.

How stakeholders are affected by business activity

Stakeholder groups affected by the activities of manufacturers may be concerned over pollution; however, since most of the UK's economy is based on providing services, it is service sector businesses that have the greatest impact on UK stakeholders. The table below gives just a few examples of positive and negative effects on stakeholder groups of business activity.

Examples of positive effects of business activity on stakeholders	Examples of negative effects of business activity on stakeholders
Businesses that provide activities for small children and their parents, bringing people together	Pollution of the body caused by over-processed foods
Specialist restaurants that give people a taste of home or the chance to eat out in a way that suits their diet/lifestyle	Prejudice created by some newspapers and their online sites
Shops that focus on organic meat and produce, giving an outlet to suppliers producing these	Treatment of staff trapped in low-wage, insecure, zero-hour contract jobs

How stakeholders impact business activity

While many stakeholder groups may try to influence business decision making and activities, few will succeed in creating major change in what businesses do. Occasionally, **pressure groups** that gain enough popular support can influence the way a firm operates – for example, convincing a business to use only Fairtrade suppliers or pay a decent wage. More often, the gentle pressure that many stakeholders apply can prevent businesses behaving in outrageous ways. Certainly, few businesses can afford to completely ignore the wishes of all stakeholder groups.

Pressure group: an organisation formed to put forward a particular viewpoint, such as promoting organic farming.

Exam tip

For most businesses, the owners or shareholders are likely to be the most influential stakeholder group. After all, it is they who own the business, having invested their own capital and, ultimately, in the case of a limited company, it is the shareholders who can replace the directors if they are unhappy about the way they are running the business.

Possible conflicts between stakeholder groups

Remembering the objectives of different stakeholders shown in the table on the previous page, it is clear that there will be times that the objectives of one stakeholder group will clash with those of another. Often the desire of shareholders to receive greater dividends, driven by more profit, will clash with the hope of employees to receive more generous pay, since higher pay pushes up costs and reduces profit.

Now test yourself

1 How might the interests of shareholders and the local community conflict if Tesco plan to open a new store near a busy local road junction?
2 State two things that a supplier may expect from a business.
3 Give an example of a situation where the needs of customers of McDonald's may conflict with the needs of those living close to a branch of McDonald's.

Answers on page 105

1.5.2 Technology and business

Technological change affects what businesses sell and how they produce and provide their products and services. Although less obvious to consumers, new ways of doing things can allow firms to offer a better service or lower their costs significantly. However, many recent technological developments have directly affected the way firms interact with their customers. Four major types of technology are detailed below.

Types of technology used by business

REVISED

E-commerce

Buying online has had a massive impact in some industries and little impact on others. Some markets are suited to the convenience and speed that **e-commerce** offers when buying a standardised product. In other markets, businesses cannot offer the speed of delivery that creates convenience for consumers. The graph shows how important e-commerce has become at Domino's Pizza over the last few years.

In other markets, e-commerce is less relevant; note that less than 5 per cent of food groceries sold in the UK are sold via e-commerce.

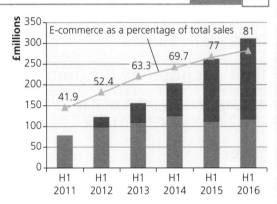

Growth of e-commerce at Domino's Pizza
(source: Domino's interim accounts 2011–16)

Advantages of e-commerce	Disadvantages of e-commerce
Enables a small business to start up from a back bedroom, testing the market before spending a lot on offices and staff.	In many sectors, winner takes all (e.g. Amazon in book sales). Dominant (monopoly) businesses rarely serve customers well in the long term.
Enables a small business to sell to the world without needing an expensive overseas sales and distribution set-up.	Dubious environmentally as there are large numbers of van deliveries and returns ('wrong size', 'not sure I like it'); this is surely a carbon-loaded way of trading.
Provides scalability; that is, you can finance faster growth than is true of old-style retail or service businesses (e.g. the growth of ASOS).	For first-movers websites and apps work well, but it is very difficult for late-arrival competitors to make themselves seen and heard by the market and it creates issues regarding monopoly.
Use of social media makes it possible to build a relationship with customers even though you do not meet them physically.	Some customers effectively blackmail businesses (e.g. 'give me a free bottle of wine or I'll give you a bad write-up on Twitter/TripAdvisor').

Social media

The main use of **social media** by business is for promotional activities. From sponsored Instagram posts to paid-for endorsements by vloggers and Twitter users, businesses see social media as a new channel through which they can directly push their messages to consumers.

> **E-commerce**: selling online rather than in a physical one-to-one transaction. An important part of e-commerce is m-commerce, meaning commerce using apps/smartphones rather than websites/PCs.
>
> **Social media**: interactive channels of communication via words, pictures or videos such as blogs, Facebook and Instagram.

Digital communication

Although social media allows communication to take place digitally, the major communication development for businesses of the last 30 years has been the invention of email, allowing instant written communication to enhance communication both within a business and with external stakeholders.

Payment systems

Payment systems such as PayPal are the drivers for e-commerce, giving people the confidence in the security of their payment details to be shared with the businesses they want to buy from via the internet. Without online payment systems in which consumers feel confident, e-commerce would grind to a halt.

> **Digital communication**: messages or conversations conducted via email, text or social media messaging services.
>
> **Payment systems**: ways of paying electronically, such as PayPal.

How technology influences business activity

REVISED

Although technology affects almost every area of business, the three main areas of focus are detailed below.

Sales

New products, such as games consoles and cars, can be created that are technologically more advanced (i.e. better quality and higher performance) and so more attractive to customers. Businesses that compete based on technologically superior products must employ experts who are able to work at the cutting edge of technology, and ahead of their rivals.

It is not just what is sold that affects sales, however. The processes involved in selling can change as a result of technology. For example, e-commerce has revolutionised the way that takeaway food is sold and delivered to customers.

Costs

The use of social media and other online methods, such as Google AdWords to target promotional materials to potential customers, offers businesses the chance to get more from the amount they spend on promotion. Meanwhile, businesses can use the internet to shop around to find cheaper suppliers and sources of materials, again driving costs down and profits up.

Marketing mix

Technology impacts on all 4Ps, as shown by the following examples.
- **Product** – Improved technology can enhance a product, allowing it to gain more market share.
- **Price** – Prices may need to be more competitive as consumers now find it easier to compare prices using the internet.
- **Promotion** – Digital marketing methods have allowed firms to target customers more effectively.
- **Place** – For many firms 'place' is the route taken by the product. Consumers buy the product via a business's website and it is then delivered to them directly. Physical retailers disappear from the process.

Now test yourself

TESTED

1 What is the main way that businesses use social media?
2 How has technology affected the process of selling pizza?
3 How can technology allow a business to find cheaper materials?

Answers on page 105

1.5.3 Legislation and business

The purpose of consumer protection legislation

REVISED

A **consumer's rights** are protected by **consumer protection legislation**. The **legislation** exists to ensure that consumers are not deceived or taken advantage of by the businesses they interact with. The three major issues covered are:

- preventing harm caused when the supplier knows more than the consumer (perhaps about the side-effects of using their product)
- preventing harm caused when the consumer is misled or lied to (perhaps about the quality of the product)
- preventing exposure to unsafe or unhealthy products.

The two most important pieces of consumer protection legislation are the Consumer Rights Act 2015 and the Trade Descriptions Act 1968.

Consumer Rights Act 2015

Key features of this Act are:

- Goods must be fit for the purpose for which they are sold, so free from defects, safe and durable.
- The buyer has the right to get their money back if the product is not fit for purpose, or to have it repaired at the seller's expense.
- The person responsible for correcting any problem is the seller (shop), not the manufacturer.

Trade Descriptions Act 1968

This Act is designed to prevent misleading claims being made about products, in particular when they are advertised. Key features are:

- It is an offence for a trader to use false or misleading statements.
- It is an offence to misleadingly label goods and services.
- The Act carries criminal penalties and can therefore lead to a jail sentence.

Other consumer protection legislation includes:

- The **Consumer Credit Act 1974** (updated in 2014) states that every item sold on credit must have a clear indication of the APR – the annualised percentage interest rate – being charged.
- The **Weights and Measures Act 1985** (updated in 2006) deals with ensuring that the quantity advertised is that which is actually sold.
- The **Food Safety Act 1990** is designed to prevent illness caused by food poisoning and focuses on hygienic staff, premises and products.

> **Consumer rights**: laws that empower the consumer to demand certain minimum standards from every business supplier.
>
> **Consumer protection legislation**: acts of parliament that are intended to protect customers from misleading or dangerous practices by companies.
>
> **Legislation**: laws passed by acts of parliament; breaking these laws may result in a fine or even a prison sentence.

> **Exam tip**
>
> Only the first two Acts shown here (Consumer Rights Act and Trade Descriptions Act) will be tested in your exam. The others are there to remind you that there are plenty of laws that businesses have to abide by.

The purpose of employment legislation

REVISED

Although many firms see employees as a valuable asset to be treated well, retained and developed, others may exploit staff. Employment laws are in place to prevent the exploitation of staff and to ensure that all staff are treated equally and fairly.

The four main areas covered by employment legislation are outlined on the next page.

Recruitment

The focus of legislation relating to recruitment is on equal opportunities for all when a job is advertised. Companies must ensure that they do not show bias and instead select the best candidate for the job.

Pay

This is another area of legislation designed to ensure that employees are not discriminated against by being paid less for doing the same work. More recently, minimum wage legislation has come into force to ensure employees are paid at a fair level.

Discrimination

Although discrimination can take place when recruiting or deciding on pay, it can be particularly seen in some companies when employees are being chosen for promotion to higher levels. Legislation exists to try to prevent this type of discrimination.

Health and safety

To ensure healthy and safe working conditions for employees, health and safety law makes employers responsible for making working conditions safe.

The impact of legislation on businesses

REVISED

The goal of legislation concerning business operations is to make sure all businesses are 'playing by the same rules'. This concept is welcomed by businesses. However, many feel that legislation adds to their costs: they have to spend more money sticking to the letter of the law. The table below summarises some of the positives and negatives felt by business owners relating to legislation.

> **Red tape:** the term given to laws that (some people say) tie the hands of businesspeople, making it hard to act entrepreneurially.

Problems caused by legislation	Benefits of legislation
Too many rules means too much paperwork, which costs time and money.	At least laws make it clear what businesses can and cannot do, allowing managers to focus on other issues.
Rules can restrict initiative and creativity.	Although rules take time and money, it is not too much to prevent business success.
It is **red tape** that may not have been designed for some types of business that they still need to adhere to.	Consumer protection law is too valuable to dismiss if the consequences of doing away with it are people's deaths from unsafe cars or faulty medicines.

Now test yourself

TESTED

1 What are the two main Acts of Parliament protecting consumers in the UK?
2 State three contexts in which discrimination could take place at work.
3 What are the two main effects of legislation on businesses (one positive and one negative)?

Answers on page 105

1.5.4 The economy and business

A fundamental influence on how any business is doing is the state of the economy.

What is the economy?

REVISED

The economy is the collective term for all of the business transactions that take place in, say, the United Kingdom throughout the year. It is 'made up' of lots of companies buying and selling with each other, lots of firms selling direct to customers (some here and some abroad) and lots of money raised and spent by the government.

The impact of economic issues on businesses

REVISED

Unemployment

The effects of the total level of **unemployment** in the UK vary from company to company. Those firms that sell essentials such as toilet roll will be relatively unaffected, but those selling luxuries may face problems if unemployment rises. The table below shows the major impacts of unemployment.

> **Unemployment**: when someone of working age wants a job but cannot get one.

	Favourable for companies	Unfavourable for companies
Unemployment is low	Demand for most goods will be high, especially luxuries such as overseas holidays.	There may be labour shortages, especially in skilled work, which will make people press for higher pay.
Unemployment is high	Large numbers seeking work keeps pay down and stops staff leaving for better-paid jobs elsewhere.	Demand for luxury goods falls and manufacturers may worry about retail customers collapsing, as BHS did in 2016.

Changes in levels of consumer income

For most firms an increase in **consumer incomes** leads to an increased demand for their products, especially if those products are the sort of luxuries that people buy, or buy more of, when times are good. However, if consumer incomes fall, these same companies will see sales slump as consumers look to cut back on their spending.

A smaller number of firms sell products or services that represent cheap alternatives to products that consumers can no longer afford. For these businesses, falling consumer incomes can mean increased sales.

> **Consumer incomes**: the term given to the amount households have available to spend after income taxes have been deducted.
>
> **Inflation**: the rate of increase in the average price level.

Inflation

When **inflation** is low (2 per cent or less) businesses are generally able to manage. Inflation becomes a problem when it rises sharply (4 per cent or above), as firms could struggle to cover the rising costs of materials and supplies. Businesses may be able to increase their own prices to offset this, but they may be unsure of whether customers will be put off by a big price rise. For many years the UK government's target for inflation has been 2 per cent.

Changes in interest rates

Interest rates matter because of the number of UK consumers who have a mortgage, as well as the number of businesses that have borrowed money from banks at variable interest rates, i.e. the rate of interest paid can be changed by the bank over the course of the loan. The table below summarises the main impacts of changes in interest rates.

> **Interest rate**: the annual cost of a loan.

Effects of lower interest rates	Effects of higher interest rates
Consumers have less interest to pay on their mortgages, so can spend more on luxuries, such as leisure and holidays. This means more revenue and so more profits.	Households with mortgages cut back on their spending as they have less money left after paying for their mortgage each month, so firms will see lower revenues.
Businesses will see costs fall if they have borrowed money as interest on loans and overdrafts will be less.	Firms may face higher costs if they have borrowed money.

Government taxation

The amount that governments charge in taxes affects businesses both directly and indirectly. The direct impact is the tax that the government charges on profit, called corporation tax. If corporation tax goes up, there will be less profit to invest and share in dividends.

There are two major indirect effects of government **taxation**.
- If taxes on households rise, such as income tax or VAT, consumers cannot afford to buy as much, so business revenues will fall.
- If the UK government adds an import tax on products bought from overseas, UK importers will face higher costs, but a UK producer may find it easier to compete with products imported from elsewhere that carry the import tax.

> **Taxation**: the charges placed by the government on goods, imported goods and the incomes of individuals and companies.
>
> **Exchange rate**: the value of one currency measured by how much it will buy of another currency.

Exam tip

Rising tax is not all bad news, since more tax means more money for the government, much of which may be spent on products and services provided by businesses.

Changes in exchange rates

The value of the pound against other currencies can go up and down. This matters especially for any business that buys from abroad or sells its products abroad.

Main effects of a strong pound	Main effects of a weak pound
Imported materials and supplies are cheaper to UK businesses, reducing costs.	Imported materials and supplies are more expensive, pushing up costs.
UK consumers can buy foreign imported competitor products more cheaply.	Imported goods are more expensive for UK consumers.
UK firms will find it hard to sell their products abroad, as their products will seem more expensive for foreign customers.	UK firms will find it easier to sell their products abroad, as their products will seem cheaper for foreign customers.

Now test yourself

TESTED

1 How might revenue for a business selling luxury cars be affected by a rise in unemployment?
2 What are the two main effects that a rise in interest rates has on businesses?
3 Why do UK-based producers enjoy a weak pound?

Answers on page 105

Exam tip

If you are asked to do any exchange rate calculations:
- If converting from pounds to a foreign currency, multiply.
- If converting from a foreign currency to pounds, divide.

1.5.5 External influences

Although entrepreneurs can control many aspects of their business, the external environment is outside their control.

Business responses to changes in technology

For firms that find their product becoming outdated, a change to the way they operate may be the answer. For others a complete change of product may be needed. The table below gives several examples of responses to changes in technology.

	The action	The logic
Sainsbury's	In early 2016, Sainsbury's bought Argos for £1.3 billion.	Sainsbury's believes that Argos has better systems for 'click and collect' and, therefore, it is part of its e-commerce battle against Ocado and Waitrose.
Airbus	In May 2016, UK aircraft factories installed their first robots.	Cheaper, faster and more flexible robots, plus the challenge of increasing the output of its A320 plant by 50 per cent, have made the robots a worthwhile investment.
***The Independent* newspaper**	*The Independent* scrapped its print edition in February 2016.	With sales slumping, the Russian owner decided to close the daily and Sunday print editions; the paper is now only available online.

Business responses to changes in legislation

New legislation, which usually means extra rules for businesses to stick to, is often seen as a burden. No doubt it may increase the time taken to complete processes. Two possible responses to this are:

- hire extra staff to cope with the paperwork
- cut back, or even scrap, a whole area of the business if it can no longer operate profitably.

However, for some, new legislation can represent an opportunity. Entrepreneurs can spot opportunities to offer products and services that ease the extra burden for firms that are willing to pay others to carry out the necessary processes required by new laws.

Business responses to changes in the economic climate

With the state of the economy constantly changing, managers can have their hands full reacting to each economic change. The best firms may be able to put themselves in a position where they insulate themselves from the harshest effects of these economic changes. Some of the types of actions that can help are detailed below.

- Train skilled staff internally and find ways to use them productively even when business is slow.
- Operate across several different countries, so that a downturn in one can be offset by better times elsewhere in the world.
- Manufacturing in different parts of the world can help to lessen the effects of adverse changes in the value of the pound.
- Use the extra profits gained when times are good to invest in new machinery and equipment to permanently lower costs.
- Profits from good times can also be used to develop and launch new products that will remain popular even when times are tough.

Now test yourself

1 Explain how a newly invented production robot can boost a manufacturer's profit.
2 How might Poundland respond to forecasts of an economic downturn?
3 Why might a UK business respond to a fall in the value of the pound by hiring more staff?

Answers on page 105

Summary

Businesses have many stakeholders, each with slightly different things they expect from the business.

Stakeholders may be able to influence the way that businesses operate.

Often different stakeholder groups may have conflicting objectives.

The four main types of technology used by business are:
● e-commerce
● social media
● communications technology
● payment systems.

Technology tends to have major effects on a business's:
● sales
● costs
● marketing mix.

The two main types of legislation that affect businesses are:
● consumer protection
● employee protection.

Consumer protection legislation focuses on quality and consumer rights.

Employee protection legislation focuses on recruitment, pay, discrimination and health and safety.

The main aspects of the economic environment that affect businesses are:
● unemployment
● changing levels of consumer income
● inflation
● changes in interest rates
● government taxation
● changes in exchange rates.

Major external influences on business are:
● changes in the economic climate
● changes in technology
● changes in legislation.

Exam practice

1 State two stakeholders for Tesco. (2)
2 State one objective of each stakeholder mentioned in your answer to question 1. (2)
3 Outline how e-commerce helps a business to reduce its fixed running costs. (2)
4 Outline one major use of social media by businesses. (2)
5 Which two of the following are examples of employee protection laws? (2)
   a) Consumer Credit Act
   b) Trade Descriptions Act
   c) Equality Act
   d) Weights and Measures Act
   e) Equal Pay Act
6 Outline one effect of an increase in unemployment on a business selling foreign holidays. (2)
7 Outline one impact of a decrease in interest rates on a business planning to expand. (2)
8 Outline one effect of an increase in the value of the pound on a UK firm that exports to foreign markets. (2)

Answers on page 110

Topic 2.1 Growing the business

2.1.1 Methods of business growth

Growing a business is especially important when the market you are in is growing. Without growth, your firm becomes less significant and may struggle to maintain a foothold in the market, as retailers no longer wish to sell your brand.

Internal (organic) growth

The safest way to grow a business is to do more of what you are already successfully doing. Ideally this **organic growth** can be funded using profits already generated and can happen at a steady pace, without the risks of sudden, huge changes in size. There are two basic ways to grow organically: new products and new markets.

New products

Most businesses begin with one product idea. Growth can come from finding other, related products that can also be launched, boosting the product range on offer.

More growth may be prompted by a genuinely **innovative** product, one that brings something completely new to the market. This is likely to come as a result of successful investment in **research and development**.

> **Organic growth**: growing from within the business, such as creating and launching successful new products.
>
> **Innovation**: bringing a new idea to the market.
>
> **Research and development (R&D)**: the scientific research and technical development needed to come up with successful new products.

New markets

The easiest way to understand the idea of entering new markets is to define markets geographically. So a UK business that wants to enter new markets may expand overseas and begin trying to sell their products in foreign markets. This is clearly a route to growing revenues, without developing new products. The major challenges associated with entering new international markets are:

- promoting an unknown brand in a market you don't yet know or understand
- understanding the local distribution system – part of the 'Place' element of the marketing mix that may be radically different in other countries
- building a management team and recruiting staff in a new country.

New markets do not have to be overseas though.

Targeting a different type of customer can be a way to access a new market. The key will be to change the marketing mix. For example, a deodorant that was aimed at women may have all four elements of its marketing mix adjusted so that it can be launched to also target men.

Another opportunity to enter new markets may come from the use of technology. New methods of promotion, using social media or other online methods, can open up new markets, while adding e-commerce or m-commerce may allow new markets to be tackled.

> **Exam tip**
>
> Although most students are aware that entering a new market is difficult, few can clearly explain why. Make sure you are clear on these practical problems that a business must overcome if it is to successfully enter a new market.

External (inorganic) growth

Takeovers

It is possible to buy a whole business. All that needs to happen is that one firm buys the shares of the other. To do this, the shareholders of the business must be persuaded to sell their shares. This will be done by offering them a generous price per share. Once the takeover bidder owns more than 50 per cent of the shares, they have effective control of the business. Sometimes an unwanted takeover can generate negative feelings – for example, 'Now they've bought us, they're going to come in and tell us to change the way we do things!' – but takeovers do offer the following benefits as a method of growth:

- Substantial growth can be achieved 'overnight'.
- The combined business has more power in negotiations with suppliers and customers.
- Duplicated jobs and processes can be eliminated, cutting the total cost of running the combined operation.

> **Inorganic (external) growth**: growing by buying up other businesses or by merging with a business of roughly equal size.

Merger

A **merger** brings similar benefits to a takeover, but without the potentially negative feelings of an unwanted takeover. However, unlike a takeover – where the management of the business doing the takeover will be the leaders after the deal – mergers can lead to tensions between managers from the two previously separate businesses.

> A **merger** happens when two businesses of roughly equal size agree to come together to form one big business.

Financing growth

Whether growth occurs organically or inorganically, it is likely to need funding to:

- carry out R&D and launch new products
- research and launch in new markets
- take over another business
- merge previously separate organisations.

Typical sources of finance for growth split into two categories: using money that is already in the business (internal sources) or attracting new money from external sources.

Internal sources

Retained profit

If a business makes a profit after deducting all of its costs and paying tax, some of that money may be retained in the business rather than being paid out as dividends. Money that is retained in the business is perhaps the safest source of finance for growth. It has no cost associated, but the quantities involved may mean that raising the amounts for major growth may take many years to accumulate.

Selling assets

If a business has assets it no longer needs, or a part of a larger business that is underperforming, it may choose to sell those assets to raise cash to finance its planned growth. If assets, especially property, are still needed, it may be possible to sell them and immediately lease them back. This raises a lump sum of cash, but may work out more expensive with rent to be paid every month on something that had been owned before.

> **Typical mistake**
>
> Be careful about suggesting that selling assets is a way of funding growth. Most growing businesses want more assets, not fewer. Look out for a company that is growing by doing something different from its past; this does suggest there will be un-needed assets that can now be sold to finance new ventures.

External sources

Although internal sources may be safer, many firms will need to look for outside sources as they cannot raise enough funds to finance their planned growth internally.

Becoming a plc

A private limited company can issue and sell shares to friends, family and associates in order to raise capital. However, there is likely to be a limit to the amount that can be practically raised from friends and family, meaning that a wider audience may be needed to buy extra shares.

For this reason, a **public limited company (plc)** is the business ownership type best suited for growing a company. Once it has become a plc, a business can 'float' (sell) its shares on the Stock Exchange, to the general public. This allows the business to raise far more **share capital**.

The table below summarises key advantages and disadvantages of becoming a plc.

Advantages	Disadvantages
It provides a sudden, possibly huge, injection of share capital into the business.	A sudden injection of a lot of money can tempt managers to be too ambitious, e.g. SuperGroup plc, which grew too fast after its 2010 flotation.
It is an excellent source of capital for a rapidly expanding business (safer than borrowing from big banks).	Suddenly selling so many shares means the founder's holding may fall below 50 per cent, therefore losing control.
'Going public' raises the profile of the business (perhaps making it easier to win big contracts from big companies).	The higher profile means shareholders and the media critique each quarter's results, perhaps encouraging short-term decision making.

> **Public limited company (plc):** a company with at least £50,000 of share capital that can advertise its shares to outsiders and is, therefore, allowed to float its shares on the stock market.
>
> **Flotation:** the term used to describe the process of listing company shares on the stock market, allowing anyone to buy the shares. This means the price can float freely (up and down).
>
> **Share capital:** money provided to a business by shareholders in return for a share in the ownership of the business.

Loan capital

Borrowing from banks is the most common source of finance used to grow businesses. Although interest will be charged and the loan must also be repaid over time, if the growth generates higher profits, these extra cash outflows should be manageable. If the growth fails to generate extra profit, it may force the business under.

Now test yourself

1 What are the two main options available to a firm planning to grow organically?
2 Identify three benefits of using takeover as a method of growth.
3 State two internal sources of finance that could be used to finance growth.

Answers on page 105

2.1.2 Changes in business aims and objectives

Why business aims and objectives change

Market conditions

Over time, especially as a business grows and targets wider and different markets, the competitors they need to deal with change. If the business's goals fail to adapt in order to tackle the new landscapes they face, they are likely to die out. Often this can mean that a growing business's focus changes from the original product or market they started with in order to avoid strong competitors.

Technology

As technology has enabled the growth in e-commerce, so business objectives have embraced the opportunities to target wider geographical markets. Change in technology relating to how products are made can shift a firm's manufacturing focus onto harnessing any technological developments that enable them to cut costs or produce innovative products.

Performance

Success will usually be based on the financial performance of a business. Should profits slide for any sustained period of time, the business may need to adjust its objectives to focus on correcting the cause of poor financial performance. This may involve an objective of cost reduction or aiming to boost revenues.

Legislation

Changes to the laws that affect business can offer opportunities, for example to cash in on helping others abide by those laws, or threats, for example if the laws stop a business doing what it has done in order to grow. Whichever is the case, the likelihood is that a change in law will force a business to adjust the targets it sets itself, finding new ways to sustain growth and success.

Internal reasons

If the people leading a business change, they may adjust the business's overall objectives, believing they have a better direction for the firm than the previous bosses. This may be due to:

● different backgrounds – if a marketing specialist takes over from a boss with an engineering background
● different beliefs about what is success – if a new boss believes there is lots of potential for more profit
● a new perspective on what the firm could do – perhaps a new boss can see opportunities that needed imagination the old boss didn't have.

How business aims and objectives change

Focus on survival or growth

Survival and growth are at opposite ends of a range of business objectives. For a business that has been struggling to maintain profits for a period, objectives may need to recognise that they have problems serious enough to threaten their survival, meaning a total focus on simply surviving becomes the goal. For other businesses that have enjoyed success when starting up, there may come a time when growth is the sensible next step.

Entering or exiting markets

Especially when a market starts to grow rapidly, as China has done in recent years, entering a new market may be a sensible objective, allowing a firm to boost its success by selling to new customers. However, changing competitive environments in some markets, such as the arrival of a dominant new competitor, may force firms to focus on withdrawing from markets in which they cannot successfully compete.

Growing or reducing the workforce

Linked once more to the idea of success or struggle, a business may need to adjust the size of its workforce.
● Cut staff to save money if the business is struggling or exiting markets.
● Increase the workforce when growth is being pursued as an objective.

Increasing or decreasing the product range

Offering a wider range of products can be a useful way to boost sales; more products gives you more chance of meeting new customers' needs. This is a popular driver for organic growth. However, for some firms, especially those looking to become more efficient, ditching less successful products allows them to cut costs and maintain revenue from a smaller range of more successful products.

> **Exam tip**
>
> Remember that making staff redundant usually carries a short-term cost as they will be entitled to redundancy pay linked to their salary and length of service.

> **Exam tip**
>
> Trying to manage a wider range of products increases the challenge faced by managers; with more to keep an eye on there is a greater danger that mistakes could be made.

Now test yourself

TESTED ☐

1 State two ways in which a struggling business may adjust its objectives to try to turn the business round.
2 If a phone business develops a brand new type of hyper-detailed camera for their phones, how might their objectives change?
3 What might be the causes of a decision by Asda to close all its supermarkets and only sell online?

Answers on page 106

2.1.3 Business and globalisation

Impact of globalisation on business

REVISED ☐

Over the past 50 years, international trading has become more common. This has had several impacts on UK businesses.

Imports

The increase in international trading has allowed companies from overseas to access the UK market more easily. This means that UK companies face far more competition from **imports** than they did 50 years ago. For many, this has led to closure; for all, it has meant the need to get better at what they do so they can still outcompete international rivals in the UK.

> **Imports**: goods or services bought from overseas companies.

Buying from overseas can offer UK businesses the chance to import materials and components that:
● may not be available in the UK
● may be cheaper from abroad
● may be of a better quality if imported.

Exports

The flip-side to more imports is that UK businesses now find it easier to export their products to foreign markets for sale. This is the result of fewer barriers to trade and cheaper international transport and communication links. The result is that the best UK companies can now sell to far more customers than 50 years ago; they are selling to a global market with, potentially, billions of customers.

Changing business locations

For UK businesses, **globalisation** has allowed them to sell worldwide. Despite improvements in transport, moving products from the UK all around the world can be too expensive or take too long. The result is that the most successful UK manufacturers have set up factories around the world, allowing them to better serve these foreign markets. In some cases, UK companies have stopped manufacturing in the UK altogether, tempted by the lower costs of manufacturing in other parts of the world.

Multinationals

As described above, a firm selling in many countries may need to set up bases in different countries. The result has been a growth in the number of **multinational** businesses operating. The key issues raised by the growth in multinationals include:
- increased power of multinationals, even when dealing with national governments
- scope for multinationals to avoid paying tax in some countries
- the role played by multinationals in developing economies: encouraging local businesses and improving local transport and communication networks.

> **Globalisation**: the increasing tendency for countries to trade with each other and to buy global goods, such as Coca-Cola, or services, such as Costa Coffee.
>
> **Multinational**: a business that has production facilities in several countries.

Typical mistake

A business that makes things in the UK then sells them abroad is not a multinational, simply a UK-based exporter. Multinationals have operating bases in more than one country.

Barriers to international trade

REVISED

Although international trade occurs more than ever before, there are still some barriers to trade between countries. The two key barriers are explained below.

Tariffs

Some governments, looking to raise taxes and protect businesses in their own country, may decide to charge **tariffs** on some or all imports to their country. Tariffs have the following effects:
- They protect home producers by making imports artificially expensive, making imports less attractive to consumers.
- They increase the cost of living for consumers, leaving everybody worse off.
- They prevent the growth of international trade/globalisation.

> **Tariffs**: taxes charged only on imports.

Trading blocs

When a group of countries agree to trade freely between themselves, businesses in those countries can treat consumers in the other **trade bloc** countries as they would their domestic customers; there will be taxes to pay on products traded within the bloc. However, being outside a trading bloc makes exporting to those countries harder since they may well impose tariffs on products they import. This is why most UK exporters are concerned about the impact of Brexit on their sales in the EU.

The EU is not the only trading bloc; the three largest blocs are briefly explained in the table below.

> **Trade bloc**: a group of countries that have agreed to have free trade within external tariff walls.

Name of the trading bloc	Trading bloc members	Main features of the bloc
EU (European Union)	27 members (after Britain's withdrawal) led by Germany and France	Free movement of goods and labour with a single market backed by common EU-wide legislation
ASEAN (Association of South East Asian Nations)	Ten members including Thailand and Vietnam, but excluding China	Free movement of goods; started in 1965 with five members; members have enjoyed high economic growth
NAFTA (North American Free Trade Association)	America, Canada and Mexico	Free movement of goods; just three members; two rich and one much less so (Mexico)

How businesses compete internationally

REVISED

Increased globalisation has opened up foreign markets to businesses and this has meant that firms must get used to competing with international rivals, rather than just domestic competitors. Competing internationally is likely to involve one or both of the actions below.

Use of the internet and e-commerce

Even small businesses are able to reach foreign customers with relative ease using the internet. Websites know no national boundaries, so a business with a website can be accessed by anyone on the planet. This means that if the business uses e-commerce, enabling sales to be made through their website, they may reach customers from all over the world.

Changing the marketing mix

Competing internationally is likely to involve adjusting one or more of the 4Ps in the marketing mix. This will allow a business to better meet the differing needs of customers in the different national markets in which they are trying to compete.

- **Product** – This may need to be adjusted to suit local climates, tastes or fashions. These adjustments may add to total costs, but should prove worthwhile if they tempt customers to buy.
- **Price** – A product's reputation may be stronger in some countries than others, allowing the product to be sold for more in countries where it is highly valued. Most multinationals will set prices country by country depending on local conditions.
- **Promotion** – Adverts are likely to need to be adjusted to suit different local tastes and trends.
- **Place** – Distribution channels differ from country to country. Perhaps most significant are the varying levels of e-commerce globally, ranging from close to 20 per cent of retail sales in Asia to around 2 per cent in Africa. Selling through a website may not be viable in some markets.

> **Now test yourself**
>
> 1 State three possible impacts of globalisation on a UK food manufacturer.
> 2 Briefly explain why UK car manufacturers are fearful of the UK leaving the EU.
> 3 How might a UK car manufacturer need to change their product to suit markets in the Middle East?
>
> Answers on page 106
>
> TESTED

2.1.4 Ethics, the environment and business

Few would argue that businesses should try to avoid harming the **environment** and should try to behave in a morally correct way at all times. However, business actions tend to be driven by the need to make profit to keep shareholders happy.

> **Environment**: the condition of the natural world that surrounds us, which is damaged when there is pollution.

How ethical considerations impact on business

REVISED

When making a decision that will impact on a business, managers will consider a range of factors, one of which will be the **ethics** of the decision. **Ethical considerations** are not limited to a business's management, however; even shop-floor staff make decisions (should I tell the customer the dress looks great on them, just so they buy it?), which can raise ethical issues.

> **Ethics**: weighing up decisions or actions on the basis of morality, not personal gain.
>
> **Ethical considerations**: thinking about ethics, which may lead to morally valid decisions or to the manipulation of customer attitudes (that is, pretending to be ethical).

At the heart of any debate relating to business and ethics is the belief that there is a trade-off between profit and ethics. In other words, choosing to behave in the 'right' way may reduce profit. Examples of this trade-off include:

- cutting costs by doing fewer safety checks on equipment
- cutting costs by using sub-standard materials in a product
- reducing the size of a chocolate bar to cut materials costs, but charging the same price
- putting sweets for kids next to supermarket checkouts to boost sales but which will damage kids' teeth.

In each case, there is a trade-off, where a business has behaved in a way that increases profit, but at a cost of behaving in a less ethical way.

Some business managers believe that this trade-off need not exist, since ethical behaviour helps to attract customers who prefer to buy from businesses with high ethical standards, as shown by the diagram on the right.

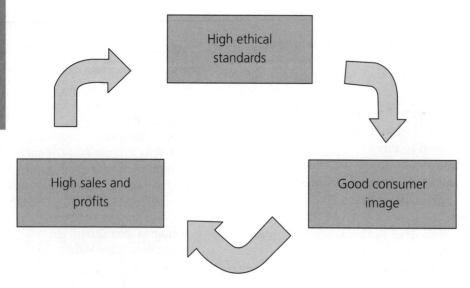

The link between ethics and profit

Now test yourself and Exam practice answers can be found on page 104 onwards

How environmental considerations impact on business

REVISED

Major **environmental considerations** facing businesses relate to recycling and energy sources:

- cutting CO_2 emissions
- relying on renewable sources of energy
- using only recycled materials in products and for packaging
- recycling any waste generated in production.

Some businesses are founded on environmentally sound principles, such as recycling businesses or the makers of wind turbines. However, for other businesses, as with ethics, there can be a trade-off between the environmental, or **sustainable**, option and the profitable option:

- Renewable sources of energy may cost more than energy generated from fossil fuels.
- Recyclable materials may cost more to use than non-recyclables.
- Recycling waste may be more expensive than dumping it.
- Investing in electric-powered delivery vehicles may be more expensive than diesel-fuelled trucks.

Once more, some businesses find a way to avoid the trade-off, either by using their environmental credentials to justify a higher selling price or by attracting new environment-conscious customers.

> **Environmental considerations**: factors relating to 'green' issues, such as sustainability and pollution.
>
> **Sustainability**: whether or not a resource will inevitably run out in the future; a sustainable resource will not.

Impact of pressure group activity on business

REVISED

Pressure groups often act as a kind of conscience for businesses. They will nag, pressure or campaign to make businesses behave ethically and/or in an environmentally responsible manner. Particular areas of focus in recent years have been:

- Greenpeace, which campaigns to stop the promotion of diesel cars and to stop drilling for oil in the Arctic
- Corporate Watch, which has campaigned for workers' and communities' rights, particularly in less economically developed countries
- PETA (People for the Ethical Treatment of Animals), which has led campaigns to ban the use of animal furs in clothing
- Searchlight, which campaigns against racism.

Pressure groups may well prevent businesses from choosing the more profitable option and taking the ethical or environmental option instead, but only when they find out about a business choice and only when they can gather enough public support to convince the business to take the better option.

> **Pressure group**: an organisation founded to achieve a specific objective – for example, Surfers Against Sewage.

Now test yourself

TESTED

1 What may be considered unethical about a business saving money by cutting back on safety checks?
2 Why may a business designing packaging for a new product choose a non-sustainable material?
3 State two major environmental issues relevant for most businesses.

Answers on page 106

Summary

Growth can be organic or inorganic.

Organic growth can come from launching new products or selling to new markets.

Inorganic growth can involve a merger or a takeover.

Finance for growth can come from internal sources or external sources.

Internal sources of finance for growth are retained profit or sale of assets.

External sources of finance for growth are issuing new shares or loan capital.

Business aims and objectives may change due to:
● changing market conditions
● changing technology
● changing performance
● changing legislation
● internal reasons.

Typical changes to business aims and objectives may involve:
● focus on survival or growth

● entering or exiting markets
● growing or reducing the workforce
● increasing or decreasing the product range.

The major impacts of globalisation on businesses are:
● imports
● exports
● changing business location
● multinationals.

Barriers to international trade are:
● tariffs
● trading blocs.

Competing internationally is likely to involve use of e-commerce and changing the marketing mix.

Many businesses recognise trade-offs between:
● ethics and profit
● environmental and sustainability considerations and profit.

Major environmental issues for businesses to consider are recycling and sustainability.

Exam practice

1 Which two of the following are methods of inorganic growth? (2)
  a) Selling new products
  b) Entering new markets
  c) Merger
  d) Takeover
2 Which two of the following are *not* common methods of financing growth? (2)
  a) Overdraft
  b) Retained profit
  c) Bank loan
  d) Issuing new shares
  e) Government grant
3 Outline why a change in business performance may lead to a change in business objective. (2)
4 Explain why a business may change its objective to reducing the size of the workforce. (3)
5 Outline two ways in which globalisation has affected UK shoe manufacturers. (4)
6 State two barriers to international trade. (2)
7 Define business ethics. (1)

Answers on page 110

ONLINE

2.2.1 Product

At the heart of the marketing mix is product. The product must match the needs of the target market, otherwise it simply will not sell. To ensure the product meets the needs of the target market, companies must identify the priorities of their target customers. A helpful tool for this is the design mix.

The design mix

REVISED

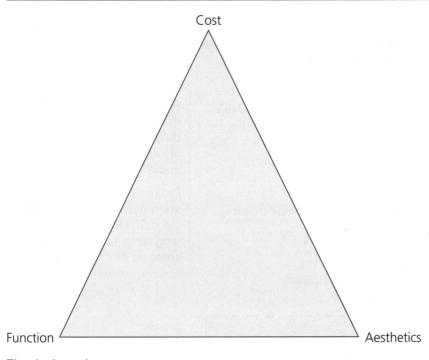

Cost

Function

Aesthetics

The design mix

Using the pyramid-shaped design mix helps the business make decisions on what mix of the three priorities (**function, aesthetics, cost**) its target market expects to see from their product.

> **Typical mistake**
>
> The design mix is a process of compromise. Very few products will be at one of the three corners, most will be somewhere near the middle of the triangle, but closer to one corner than the others.

> **Function**: how well the product or service works for the customer; for example, are the beds comfortable at a hotel; does the smartphone take sharp photos?
>
> **Aesthetics**: how things appeal to the senses; do they look great, smell good, feel nice, sound solid (the 'ker-lunk' of a BMW door shutting) and taste great?
>
> **Cost**: making the product cheaply enough for it to be profitable.

Product differentiation

REVISED

Finding a way to make your product seem different from rivals' is a crucial role of the design process. If consumers believe your product to be different from others, loyalty will follow, as no other substitute quite fits the bill like yours. Not only will customers develop a loyalty to your product, it will also give more freedom over what price to charge.

> **Product differentiation**: the extent to which consumers see your product as different from its rivals'.

Product life cycle

REVISED

The approach to marketing should be determined by trends in the product's sales, often examined using the **product life cycle** model. The model consists of four phases, detailed in the table below.

Stage of life cycle	Characteristics
Introduction	After spending money on research and development, the product is launched: the focus must be on raising awareness it exists. Sales are likely to be low and rise only slowly. Advertising will be informative and distribution only limited. The product may be unique and therefore sold at a high price.
Growth	This is the stage when sales start to grow as far more people become aware of the product. Price remains high, so with growing sales comes profit.
Maturity	Sales growth flattens and competitors emerge, trying to copy the product idea. Now promotion will focus on differentiating your brand. However, sales are at their highest, so profit should be strong.
Decline	As sales and profits start to fall because the product no longer meets consumers' needs, prices are likely to be cut, promotional budgets slashed and distribution may focus on discount stores only.

Part of the trouble with the product life cycle is that different products have different lengths of life cycle – for example, while Cadbury's Dairy Milk may still be going strong after 100 years, fidget spinners may not be around by the time you read this.

Extension strategies

Some companies will try to prevent entering the decline phase by using an **extension strategy**. Typical techniques involved include:

- finding new uses for the product
- changing the appearance, format or packaging
- encouraging customers to use the product more frequently
- adapting the product – 'new and improved'.

> **Product life cycle**: a theory that every product goes through the same four stages of introduction, growth, maturity and decline.
>
> **Extension strategy**: an attempt to prolong sales of a product for the medium to long term, to prevent it from entering its decline phase.

Typical mistake

An extension strategy must be something that is expected to prolong life by several years. Short-term offers, such as buy one get one free, are not strategic.

Now test yourself

TESTED

1 What are the three parts of the design mix?
2 What are the four stages of the product life cycle?
3 State two typical types of extension strategy.

Answers on page 106

2.2.2 Price

Getting the price right or wrong can make or break a product. The right price is likely to be affected by:
- the rest of the marketing mix
- technology
- competition
- market segment
- product life cycle.

Pricing strategies

REVISED

In broad terms, there are two basic pricing strategies:
- pricing low for high volume but with low **profit margins**
- pricing high for low volume but high profit margins.

> **Profit margin**: profit as a percentage of the selling price (one unit) or as a percentage of total sales revenue (for the business as a whole).

> **Exam tip**
>
> Low price need not mean low profit. Selling hundreds of millions of products, each of which makes a few pence of profit, is very profitable for some microchip manufacturers.

Influences on pricing strategies

REVISED

Technology

Technology, specifically e-commerce, has tended to drive prices down. As the internet makes comparing prices for products far easier, companies tend to need to advertise lower prices, particularly for online buyers. What makes this possible is the lower fixed costs associated with e-commerce compared to traditional retailing; with no need for a high street store, profit can be made at a lower price for e-tailers.

Competition

Close competition drives down prices. This is why companies try hard to differentiate their products from rivals. This reduces the level of effective competition, which allows prices to be raised. If there is no viable alternative to an iPhone, Apple can charge you a very high price.

Companies unable to differentiate their product successfully will end up simply following the prices set by their rivals, offering them no scope to raise prices in the event of their costs rising.

Market segments

A business selling their product to a broad, **mass market**, hoping most consumers will buy their product, are likely to need to price low. This low price strategy is feasible, as the business will be aiming for high volumes of sales, allowing their small profit margin to generate a large total amount of profit.

For a business selling a product aimed at a small market segment – a **niche market** – their strategy will be the opposite, pricing high because they hope to meet customers' needs precisely. This means that despite low sales volume, the high margin on each unit sold should generate a healthy profit.

> **Mass market**: a broad market segment that includes most consumers buying within the market.
>
> **Niche market**: a small sub-section of a larger market in which consumers share similar needs.

Product life cycle

Pricing approaches will change as a product moves through its life cycle.

Stage of life cycle	Approach to pricing
Introduction	Unique new products may charge a high introductory price to recover development costs as quickly as possible. A high price may also help to create an exclusive image. For other products, a low introductory price may be used to tempt customers to try the product.
Growth	Here, low prices may start creeping up as the product gains popularity and loyal customers, while initially high prices may start to fall to allow the less wealthy access to the product.
Maturity	Now there will be a clear focus on which price will generate the most profit, and whether a 'low price, high volume' or 'high price, low volume' strategy works best.
Decline	Most firms will cut prices of products in decline, to squeeze as many sales as possible out of a dying product. Others may look to exploit the few remaining loyal customers by pushing prices up while stocks remain.

Now test yourself

TESTED

1 What effect does product differentiation have on the price a business can charge?
2 Why might a new soft drink in the introduction phase of its life cycle be given a low price?
3 How has technology affected pricing?

Answers on page 106

2.2.3 Promotion

As examined previously, promotion is any activity that aims to promote sales of a product.

Promotional strategies

Different market segments often require different **promotional strategies**. Some of the key strategies that can be employed are looked at now.

Advertising

Using mass media such as television to advertise a product is well-suited to the mass market. Mass media allow a business to reach a huge number of customers in one go, admittedly for a high total cost, but the cost per person reached will be low.

If trying to advertise to smaller market segments, other media, perhaps digital media, make more sense, being cheaper overall, but also making it easier to target specific types of customers.

Sponsorship

Sponsorship helps to align a business with an activity whose values the brand would like to reflect. So a product looking to create an edgy, urban image may sponsor an urban music festival or sports such as skateboarding or BMX racing. A company looking to create a traditional but classy image may sponsor classical music concerts or a show-jumping event.

In some ways, sponsorship can therefore be an effective way of targeting a type of customer, as long as the market is being segmented according to hobbies or interests.

> **Typical mistake**
>
> Although some consider sponsorship to be a source of finance, it is so rarely applicable that it is usually judged wrong in an exam. Instead, sponsorship is a good example in an exam context of a method of promotion.

Branding

Strange as it sounds, the best **branding** creates a personality for a product; it attempts to 'humanise' it. The reason for doing this is to help the target market to feel that your brand 'matches' their own personality and values, or at least the personality they would like to be seen to have. The tools used to build a brand include decisions on the product – its design mix, name and packaging – in addition to the choice of promotional methods and media used and in some cases the distribution channels used.

> **Promotional strategy**: a medium- to long-term plan for communicating with your target customers.
>
> **Sponsorship**: when companies pay to have a brand associated with an iconic individual or event (usually connected with sports or the arts).
>
> **Branding**: giving your product or service a name that helps recall and recognition and gives a sense of personality.

> **Typical mistake**
>
> Never suggest that a business should advertise their products on the BBC. The BBC does not show adverts; its money comes from the licence fee, unlike commercial channels that sell advertising space to firms.

> **Exam tip**
>
> Always consider the size of the business before deciding the best way to advertise. National campaigns using mass media such as television or radio will cost hundreds of thousands of pounds, if not millions, making it way out of reach of any small business's promotional budget.

Product trials

Giving customers a free taste or extended trial of a product is used when there is a known hurdle to prevent customers making a purchase on their own. This is especially useful for food and drink products where 'taste is everything'. If the trial convinces consumers that they like the product, they may well buy it. The problem is the level of cost involved, since product trials usually involve paying people to give out the free samples. This can be a significant cost and means that trials are likely to be targeted at only small groups of customers.

Special offers

A special offer, such as buy one get one free, is likely to have an immediate impact on sales of your product but this may only be for as long as the offer is in place. The major problem is the likelihood that special offers devalue the brand in the eyes of consumers. This means special offers are rarely used by companies selling brands that are trying to project an image of high quality.

The use of technology in promotion

REVISED

Targeted advertising online

Online advertising is an effective way to target customers. As a result of the data on consumers gathered by cookies, companies can show adverts to known users of their products or choose to target customers of their competitors with advertising messages online.

The growth of online advertising is driven by the fact that UK consumers now spend an awful lot of time online, with a drift away from sitting in front of the television. Advertising spending has followed this drift to where people are: in front of a phone or tablet screen.

Viral advertising via social media

The idea behind viral advertising is that, just like the flu, the advert spreads from person to person as they share links to YouTube clips or retweet an advertising clip. For the most effective online advertising this strategy can reach tens of millions of consumers relatively cheaply, which explains the attractiveness of this strategy.

E-newsletters

Sending regular updates to customers who have shared an email address is an effective way to build customer loyalty and encourage repeat purchasing. For what is a relatively low cost, **e-newsletters** can be designed and automatically emailed to everyone in a customer database, again showing how the cheapness of some electronic methods of promotion can make them particularly attractive to small businesses with limited promotional budgets.

> **E-newsletters**: regular updates on the activities of a business sent electronically to actual or potential customers.

Now test yourself

TESTED

1 Why are product trials, where a person hands out free samples of a product to potential customers, so expensive?
2 Why are special offers a dangerous strategy to use for a high quality brand?
3 What feature do e-newsletters and viral advertising via social media share that makes them attractive to businesses?

Answers on page 106

2.2.4 Place

Methods of distribution

The three main routes that products in the UK take to move from producer to consumer are shown in the diagram below.

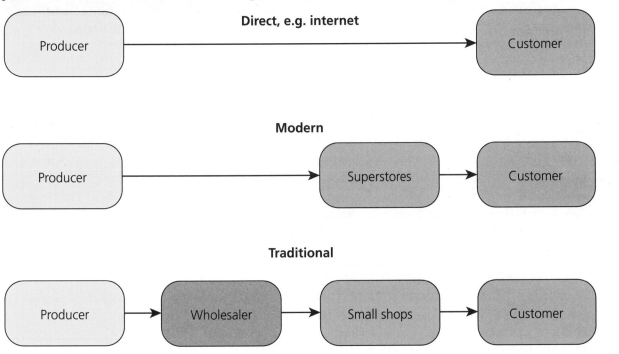

Distribution channels

At the top of the diagram is the 'direct' channel of **distribution**, where consumers buy direct from producers. This is the method used when consumers purchase via e-commerce or m-commerce.

In the middle of the diagram is the 'modern' method through which most groceries bought from UK supermarkets are distributed, with the producer delivering direct to large retailers' distribution depots.

The final channel of distribution ('traditional') involves producers delivering large quantities of their products to wholesalers who will then break down these bulky quantities to sell on in smaller batches to retailers, usually small shops.

> **Distribution:** how ownership changes as a product goes from producer to consumer.

> **Exam tip**
>
> Each time a product passes from one business to another, a little extra will be added to the selling price, to allow each firm to make a profit. This helps to explain why products bought direct from the producer can usually be purchased more cheaply.

Retailers

The main role of a **retailer** is to provide a convenient place for customers to come and look at, compare and then buy their products. This role has not disappeared despite the rise of e-tailing. The table below shows benefits and drawbacks of physical retailing for consumers.

> **Retailer**: a shop or chain of shops, usually selling from a building in a high street or shopping centre.

Advantages	Disadvantages
Customers can touch, hold, feel smell and wear products before buying. This makes it easy to compare rival products.	Going shopping is time consuming, especially when it seems important to make full comparisons (e.g. visiting lots of shops).
You can choose a lean piece of meat or a nearly ripe piece of fruit. E-commerce can't match that.	Choice can be overwhelming, leading to too much time being spent shopping.
You can take it away instantly. Not even same-day delivery can match that.	You have to carry everything. This is especially hard for anyone without a car (around 30 per cent of households).

> **Typical mistake**
>
> Never imply that launching a new product is simply a matter of persuading consumers to buy the product. Without convincing retailers to stock the product in their stores the product will not succeed (unless it can be successfully distributed directly from producer to consumer).

Since no retailers will deliberately keep empty spaces on their shelves, any new business, or a business launching a new product, will need to convince retailers to remove something from their shelves if the new product is going to gain distribution. Without retail distribution few products will be successful. To convince retailers to sell their product, producers will need to:
- show that their product offers something different
- show that they will support the product with promotional activity
- provide an acceptable level of profit for the retailer.

E-tailers

REVISED

The two main types of e-commerce are:
- direct sales from producer to consumer through the producer's website
- sales through an **e-tailer** – an electronic shop, such as ASOS.

E-tailers have the benefit of not needing to locate their physical premises in areas easily accessible by customers. This means lower rents, which helps to explain the lower prices they can charge compared to traditional retailers paying for space on high streets or in shopping centres.

> **E-tailer**: an electronic retailer; in other words purchasing electronically, either by e-commerce or, more likely these days, mobile commerce (m-commerce).

Now test yourself

TESTED

1 Which channel of distribution is used for most Mars bars sold in the UK?
2 Why might a producer make more profit by using the direct channel of distribution?
3 State two actions the producer of a brand new product may need to take to secure distribution through retailers.

Answers on page 106

2.2.5 Using the marketing mix to make business decisions

Decisions on how to market the product will have a deep influence on its chances of success. The reasons are clear.

- Get the product wrong and nobody wants to buy it.
- Get the price wrong and consumers can't afford it or it makes the product seem cheap or low quality.
- Get promotion wrong and buyers don't know the product is out there.
- Get the place wrong and potential customers can't get hold of the product.

How each element of the mix can influence others

REVISED

A good marketing mix is one where the 4Ps work in harmony. Therefore, it should be clear that a decision relating to one element of the mix may affect other Ps. Some examples are shown in the table below.

Elements of marketing mix	Effects on other Ps	
Product	Cost and features will have a major impact on Price	Type of product usually determines the distribution channel (Place)
Price	Price level will determine what type of retailers (Place) will be appropriate	Price will affect the key Promotional messages: classy for high price, value for low price
Promotion	Special offers may focus on short-term cuts to Price	Retailers (Place) will need to be informed of planned promotions to buy more stock
Place	Promotion may need to inform consumers of where to buy the product	If distribution channel involves wholesalers and retailers, this will push up Price paid by consumer

How the marketing mix can build competitive advantage

REVISED

The marketing mix is a common method through which a company can build a significant advantage over its rivals, something they do better than others that will make them more appealing to consumers than their rivals.

Product

- Features of the product that other companies cannot or do not offer give a competitive edge.
- Variations can help a firm to stand out by better enabling them to meet customers' needs with the right size, flavour or colour.
- Great quality of manufacture, using great materials, is another way that the product can give a competitive advantage.
- Design, as Apple keeps showing us, can give a real edge over rivals.

Price

- A company that can sell the cheapest product on the market has a competitive advantage.
- Even if there are cheaper similar products, if a company can set the lowest price among its closest rivals, they may be seen as the cheapest in their market niche.

> **Exam tip**
>
> Fundamentally, marketing's key role is to make a product better than its rivals' in some way. When reading a case study, ask what is the firm doing better than its rivals? If the answer is nothing, they are unlikely to be doing well.

Promotion

- Brand image can be a major advantage for a business. Despite the massive amount of investment usually needed to build a powerful and popular brand, it may be worth it if the brand is *the* brand that consumers favour above all others.
- Some companies, with the help of their advertising agencies, develop incredibly memorable adverts or advertising campaigns that provide a real competitive advantage.
- A business that harnesses technology better than any rival to understand their customers may be better able to target consumers with the right promotions and offers. This more accurate targeting can represent a genuine competitive advantage.

Place

- Getting the product into more stores than others, often due to a great team of salespeople or very generous margins offered to retailers, can give a business an edge.
- Having the product stocked in a type of store that business rivals are unable to get into can help a business stand out from their competitors.
- Better online facilities can make a company's website one that online browsers really enjoy, or designing a brilliantly functioning app can help to gain a competitive edge.

How the marketing mix can be used to implement business decisions

Once a decision has been made about a business's strategy, the marketing mix is likely to be a key part of making that strategy happen.

Company decides on an aim of growth		Set objective – boost sales by 25% in two years		**Decide on an appropriate marketing mix:** • Add extra variations to appeal to a wider market • Drop price by 5% • Use television advertising campaign to raise awareness of the brand and inform of new product variations • Increase sales team to try to get the product into 2,000 new outlets in two years

Using the marketing mix to make business decisions

Of course, these plans must be carried out: marketing departments do not just spend their time planning, they actually need to do things, like visiting retailers, buying slots to show adverts on television and developing promotional materials.

Typical mistake

Decisions on the marketing mix are not made in a vacuum. The mix must be seen as a tool for helping the business to achieve its overall aim or objective.

Now test yourself

1 Briefly explain how poor promotion can cause a new product to flop when it is released.
2 State one way in which each P can affect another P.
3 State one way in which each P can bring a competitive advantage.

Answers on page 106

Summary

A key aspect of the product is the design mix.

The design mix balances:
- economic manufacture (cost)
- aesthetics
- function.

The product life cycle has four stages:
- introduction
- growth
- maturity
- decline.

A company may use an extension strategy to prolong a product's life.

Differentiating a product helps it stand out from competitors'.

Pricing strategies may be either:
- high price, low volume
- low price, high volume.

Influences on pricing strategy include:
- technology
- market segments
- competition
- product life cycle.

Promotional strategies include:
- advertising
- sponsorship
- product trials
- special offers
- branding.

Technology can be used in promotion by:
- targeted advertising online
- viral advertising via social media
- e-newsletters.

There are three main channels of distribution:
- direct
- modern
- traditional.

Each element of the marketing mix can influence the others.

The marketing mix can provide a key source of competitive advantage.

Exam practice

1 Which two of the following are *not* part of the design mix? (2)
   a) Aesthetics
   b) Promotion
   c) Cost
   d) People
   e) Function

2 Which one of the following is *not* a stage of the product life cycle? (1)
   a) Production
   b) Decline
   c) Growth
   d) Maturity
   e) Introduction

3 Outline how the promotion of a product might change as it moves from the introduction stage of the product life cycle into the growth stage. (2)

4 Define product differentiation. (1)

5 Which one of the following is *not* a method of promotion? (1)
   a) Product trials
   b) Sponsorship
   c) Special offers
   d) Customer service
   e) Branding

6 State two ways in which businesses use technology in promotion. (2)

7 Identify what can be found between producer and consumer in the modern distribution channel. (1)

Answers on page 110

ONLINE

Topic 2.3 Making operational decisions

2.3.1 Business operations

The purpose of business operations

The operations part of the business is responsible for ensuring that customers get the products or services they buy. Whereas the marketing department's job is to create demand, operations must actually produce and deliver the product or service.

For a manufacturer, the role of operations starts with finding supplies and setting up a production line to make the product, then flows through manufacturing to delivering the product once it is made. For a service provider, operations will include the booking through to turning up and delivering the service.

Production processes

There are three fundamental types of production processes: **job, batch** and **flow**.

> **Job production**: one-off production of a one-off item for each individual customer.
>
> **Batch production**: producing a limited number of identical products.
>
> **Flow production**: continuous production of identical products, which gives scope for high levels of automation.

The table below summarises the advantages and disadvantages of each method.

	Advantages	Disadvantages/limitations
Job production	It is highly flexible and gives the customer exactly what they want. It provides satisfying work for the individual as it requires skills and flexibility.	It will always be expensive in a developed (high wage) economy. The skills may be in short supply, making it hard for the business to grow.
Batch production	It will gain some cost advantages from producing several items at once, yet will still be able to offer customer the colour/size they want.	There may be limited scope for automation, making production costs far higher than with flow production. It is not as flexible as job production.
Flow production	Flow can automate fully, making it highly cost effective (which should be good for customers as well as suppliers). Many customers value consistency and flow will provide an identical product each time.	It is likely to be expensive to set up and inflexible to use. It could be a disaster if a product life cycle proves much shorter than expected. Modern customers like to see products tailored to their specific needs.

Probably the most important goal of business operations, especially the production aspect, is to try to keep **productivity** as high as possible.
- High productivity means that any fixed costs are spread across more units of output.
- This leads to lower costs per unit.
- Lower costs per unit allow the business to still make a healthy profit even at a lower (but more competitive) selling price.

Productivity: a measure of efficiency, usually output per person per time period (for example, in 1999 Nissan UK's productivity was measured as 98 cars per worker per year).

Impacts of technology on production

REVISED

Technology can help production, by using machinery: **automation**. This is likely to boost efficiency. Recent developments in production technology, especially **robots**, can also aid **flexibility**.

Production costs

Production technology, especially robots, can help to lower production costs. They will do this in many ways, including working without breaks, working at weekends and through the night with no extra pay expected, and even working in dangerous environments where previously workers expected to be paid 'danger money'. The result of lower production costs is the ability to set lower prices, which should increase demand and make customers happy.

Automation: using machines that can operate without people.

Robots: machines that can be programmed to do tasks that can be done by humans, such as welding, spray painting and packing.

Flexibility: the ability to switch quickly and easily from one task to another.

Productivity

Replacing people with machines or robots is likely to reduce labour costs per unit. With the ability of machines to work faster, or for longer periods than humans, productivity rates rise and so production costs will be lowered. This, again, allows lower prices to be charged.

Exam tip

Note that replacing people with machines or robots has a big negative effect on cash flow in the short-term. Not only do machines need to be paid for, but staff may be entitled to a redundancy payment of several thousand pounds each.

Quality

Machines are good at consistency. Given that a key component of production quality is often producing an identical product over and over again, technology can boost this aspect of quality. In addition, technology can help to ensure that measurement of quality is made more accurate than would be possible with the human eye. This again increases the likelihood of lots of accurately made products.

Flexibility

Technology, historically, lacks flexibility. Machines may well be good at doing things one way, but cannot cope with subtle variations that consumers may be looking for. The result can be that technology reduces the flexibility a business may be able to offer. More recently, developments in production technology, notably in production robots, have focused on finding ways to make machines more flexible.

Now test yourself

TESTED

1 State two benefits of choosing to switch from job to batch production.
2 Explain one reason why a small business may not choose to use flow production.
3 List the four main ways in which technology affects production.

Answers on page 107

2.3.2 Working with suppliers

Managing stock

Ensuring that enough products are available to satisfy demand is a fundamental role of the operations section of a business. If this is to happen, they must work closely with suppliers of **stocks** and materials, as well as effectively managing the stock that is already in the business.

> **Stock(s)**: items held by a firm for use or sale – for example, components for manufacturing or sellable products for a retailer.

Bar gate stock graphs

If a business has too much in stock, they will find the cost of storing it is high and there is a danger it may go off or out of fashion before it is sold. On the other hand, too little stock runs the risk of running out and having to turn away customers who may never return.

Graphs like the **bar gate stock graph** shown here are used to help illustrate a firm's stock position.

The graph shows:
- The stock levels start at 90 units.
- Stock is gradually being used up.
- By week 4, the **buffer** level of 10 is reached.
- At the start of week 4, a batch of 80 items arrives in the business.
- This pushes the stock level back up to 90 units.

Stock management can be automated, with bar code scanners noting when stock falls below a certain level and automatically re-ordering more stock.

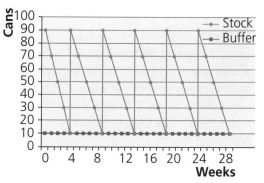

Bar gate stock graph

> **Typical mistake**
>
> Note that deliveries of new stock show as a line going straight up because a new batch arrives in one go. Stock is used gradually, so as the line falls, it moves diagonally downwards.

> **Exam tip**
>
> If the gradient of the stock line changes, it means stock is being used more quickly (steeper) or more slowly.

> **Bar gate stock graph**: a diagram to show changes in the stock level over time.
>
> **Buffer** (stock): the minimum stock level held at all times to avoid running out.
>
> **Just in Time (JIT)**: running the business with so little stock that new supplies have to arrive 'just in time' before they run out.

Just in Time

Companies that adopt **Just in Time** stock control try to operate with virtually no buffer stock, meaning that the timing of deliveries is critical. They increase their risk of running out, but save money on stock storage costs. Further advantages and disadvantages are shown in the table below.

Advantages	Disadvantages
Eliminating buffer stock cuts storage space, allowing more sales space.	There is a greater risk of running out of stock and therefore disappointing customers.
Low stock and more frequent supplier deliveries mean fresher produce.	Buying smaller quantities more often means losing out on bulk-buying discounts.
Less of the business's capital is tied up in stock.	Any mistake or misjudgement could cause out-of-stock and poorer customer service.

Procurement

The relationship between a company and its suppliers, along with the initial decision over which supplier to choose, will help to determine each of the following factors affecting **procurement**.

> **Procurement**: obtaining the right supplies from the right supplier.

Quality

If quality means that something does the job it is expected to do, then the quality of supplies is vital. Fit a faulty component inside a product and the product will not function correctly. Sell a faulty product to a customer and they will be annoyed. The quality a company expects from suppliers need not mean the very finest parts or ingredients, but all supplies must do the job they are bought to do.

Delivery

The reliability of delivery is a key factor. If a delivery:
- is late in arriving
- contains the wrong quantity
- contains the wrong product

the business may be unable to satisfy its customers or production may grind to a halt. The speed of a delivery should also be taken into account. Quicker delivery will be a benefit, so if a supplier can deliver in minutes or hours, it would be preferable to deliveries taking several days or even weeks to arrive. The cost associated with a delivery is a final factor to consider. A fast delivery might be extremely expensive.

Availability

Suppliers that cannot cope with the size or complexity of the order required will be of little use. This explains why some smaller businesses struggle to get customers from the firms they hope to supply; they need to prove that they are capable of ensuring they can always deliver the required quantities, at the required time.

> **Availability**: knowing how to get the right supplies quickly, just when you need them.

Cost

A supplier charging a lower price means lower costs for the business. This would make it easier to make a profit. However, if the lower cost supplier cannot ensure they get quality, availability and delivery right, the money saved by buying cheaper supplies may be lost as a result of:
- lost customers
- money spent fixing faults
- money spent on returns or guarantee claims.

Trust

Trust between a company and its suppliers can be crucial. Areas where this is especially important include:
- trust that payment will be made on time when credit is offered
- trust that a delivery will happen when promised
- trust that the quality and reliability of deliveries will be good
- trust that a supplier will not reveal product secrets to competitors.

> **Trust**: building a business relationship in which both sides know that the other won't let them down.

Impact of logistics and supply decisions

REVISED

The three main ways in which **logistics** and supply decisions will affect a business are:

- **Costs** – Reliable and well-priced supplies help to keep the costs of running your business under control.
- **Reputation** – If a business experiences supply problems, meaning that they do not meet customer deadlines or cannot meet demand, their reputation will be damaged.
- **Customer satisfaction** – Customers expect the product they want to be available when they want it. If a company's suppliers prevent this from happening, or their stock management is poor, they run the risk of dissatisfied customers.

> **Logistics**: ensuring that the right supplies will be ordered and delivered on time.

Now test yourself

TESTED

1. What name is given to the minimum level of stock a company aims to keep at all times?
2. How does Just in Time help businesses to save money?
3. List the five main factors to consider when choosing a new supplier.

Answers on page 107

2.3.3 Managing quality

Providing a quality product or service is fundamental to business success. The table below shows that customers judge quality in numerous ways.

	Production of goods	Production of services
Quality of initial impact	Well packaged and well presented (posh cars even need to smell new and posh)	Restaurant: food looks and smells great Hotel: room looks clean and smells fresh
Quality in usage	Few or no niggles at the start; reliable and hard wearing	Everything works well/tastes good/proves comfortable (in hotels, a great night's sleep)
Quality of after-sales service	Friendly follow-up call four weeks after purchase, any problems dealt with quickly and cheaply (preferably free)	When calling back for that lost iPhone, staff really care/look/find!

Quality is too important to be left to chance. There are two main approaches to managing quality: quality control and quality assurance.

Quality control

REVISED

Quality control relies on inspecting or checking products and service situations to try to ensure customers never experience poor quality.

Examples of how quality control can happen are:

- Factory inspectors at the end of the production line check every fifth car or carpet before it is sent to the customer.
- A head chef checks *every* plate of food before it is served.
- A feedback system that gives customers the chance to comment on their overall experience.

> **Quality control**: putting measures in place to check that the customer receives an acceptable level of quality.

The problem with quality control is it is focused on finding and correcting quality problems. The alternative approach is quality assurance.

Quality assurance

REVISED

A quality assurance system is based on preventing quality problems occurring, rather than finding and fixing them. A quality assurance system details everyone's role in ensuring quality is right first time, helping everybody to understand their own role in maintaining the highest quality standards.

Quality, cost control and competitive advantage

REVISED

Although some may suggest that quality increases costs, getting quality right can actually help to control costs.
- There is less wastage of materials.
- There will be lower labour costs if faults do not need to be fixed.
- Fewer managers will be needed to keep an eye out for problems.

So if higher quality and lower costs go hand in hand, a business that 'gets quality right' will have two significant advantages over competitors.

Now test yourself

TESTED

1 Suggest two ways in which poor quality could be seen in a restaurant.
2 How does quality assurance differ from quality control?
3 State two ways that good quality reduces costs.

Answers on page 107

2.3.4 The sales process

The process of persuading a customer to give a business some of their money in return for the product or service issued needs careful attention from any business. Few, if any, firms are in a position where customers will buy no matter how badly they are treated. So, keep customer service levels up if revenue is to stay healthy. The sales process can be split into five main sections, each of which needs consideration from a business that is looking to offer customers the best service possible.

Product knowledge

REVISED

Staff who cannot answer customers' questions about the product they sell are unlikely to make sales. To ensure that staff have strong product knowledge:
- train staff well
- retain staff, so they are experienced and really get to know products over time
- recruit people who really care about customers.

> **Product knowledge**: how well staff know the features of the products and service issues surrounding the products, such as the precise terms of Kia's seven year warranty on its new cars.

Speed and efficiency of service

REVISED

While some customers may demand exceptional levels of service (freshly ground coffee and pastries when you arrive at the hair salon), others will expect less (somebody answers the phone within 30 seconds and can help to solve your problem). The consistent expectations, however, are speed and efficiency. Nobody likes being kept waiting, so service must be delivered promptly to make sales and retain customers. However, if the cost of speed is inefficiency – somebody deals with you immediately, but can't answer your question and takes ages to find out who can – the service is again poor.

Customer engagement

REVISED

Some brands have engaged their customers successfully for many years; they almost make customers feel like they are part of an exclusive 'club', something that branding is critical to. The rise of social media, however, has taken opportunities for **customer engagement** to a new level. If a business can interact with customers daily – for example, through the social media apps on their phone – that creates a remarkably personal direct relationship.

> **Customer engagement:** the attempt to make a customer feel part of something rather than an outsider.

Responses to customer feedback

REVISED

Customer feedback comes in various forms, perhaps the three main ones being:

- direct feedback to the business, offered in person or through comments on the business's website
- word of mouth to friends and family, with customers telling people how good or bad their holiday or meal was
- comments on review sites, such as TripAdvisor.

> **Customer feedback:** comments, praise or criticisms given to the company by its customers.

Clearly, responding effectively to customer feedback implies action. If direct complaints are received, it is crucial that a business responds and tries to fix the issue(s) raised, if they are to have any chance of retaining or re-gaining customers. For example, many businesses will take the time to reply to negative customer comments left on TripAdvisor.

Post-sales service

REVISED

Fixing problems that arise after a sale is made is a final component of an effective sales process. Although the temptation to not bother with support once a customer has paid up may be great, failure to tackle post-sales problems will be a recipe for poor reputation and dwindling sales.

Now test yourself

TESTED

1 State three ways to ensure staff have good product knowledge.
2 Explain what is meant by customer engagement.
3 State three ways in which customers may provide feedback on their transaction.

Answers on page 107

Summary

Business operations is the part of a business responsible for providing the product or service.

The three main methods of production are:
- job
- batch
- flow.

Job production is the most flexible but most expensive, with flow being less flexible but producing products more cheaply.

Higher productivity leads to lower unit costs as fixed costs are spread over more units of output.

Technology has four major effects on production:
- cost
- productivity
- quality
- flexibility.

Bar gate stock graphs show stock levels, stock usage and the level of buffer stock.

Just in Time (JIT) aims to operate with no buffer stock.

Decisions on how much stock to hold need to balance the danger of running out of stock with the cost of holding stock.

Key issues to consider when choosing suppliers are:
- quality
- delivery
- availability
- cost
- trust.

Stock and procurement decisions can impact on:
- cost
- reputation
- customer satisfaction.

The two major methods of quality management are quality control and quality assurance.

Quality control focuses on identifying and correcting quality problems, whereas quality assurance focuses on preventing quality problems.

Effective quality management helps to:
- control costs
- gain competitive advantage.

The five major issues to consider in the sales process are:
- product knowledge
- speed and efficiency of service
- customer engagement
- responses to customer feedback
- post-sales service.

Exam practice

Zebra Ltd manufacture incredibly expensive luxury cuddly toys in their factory in South Wales. After several years of record profits (£2m last year), the company's directors are keen to grow. However, they are concerned about their ability to sustain a product range of eight designs, especially as their unicorn toy generates 80 per cent of current sales. They are planning to switch from batch production of the eight different designs to flow production of unicorn toys only. Setting up a flow production line for unicorns is likely to cost £35m. The line should be able to produce 5,000 toys per week. Once production is underway, the company will introduce a quality control system to maintain production standards. In addition, the company recognises the need to ensure that their sales team's product knowledge remains strong given the changes in the product range.

One director has suggested the company considers changing their material supplier. Figures for their current and possible new supplier are shown below.

	Current supplier	Possible new supplier
Cost per unit	£10	£7.50
Average delivery time	2 days	5 days
Maximum delivery possible	8,000 units	5,000 units

1. Define quality control. (1)
2. Outline one way the company can ensure the sales team's product knowledge remains strong. (2)
3. Outline one way that a bar gate stock control graph would help the company once they switch to flow production. (2)
4. Should Zebra Ltd change supplier? Justify your answer. (9)
5. Evaluate whether the switch to flow production is likely to improve profit. (12)

Answers on page 111

ONLINE

Topic 2.4 Making financial decisions

2.4.1 Business calculations

Gross profit

Gross profit is the difference between a product's selling price and what the product costs the business. Therefore, if a clothing store wants to calculate gross profit, they must deduct the cost of buying the clothes they sell from their revenue. For a manufacturer, the direct costs involved in making the product they manufacture are deducted from revenue to work out gross profit. These direct costs may include materials and components as well as the costs of running the factory.

> **Gross profit**: the amount left after the cost of buying or making a product has been deducted from revenue: gross profit = revenue − **cost of sales**.
>
> **Cost of sales**: the name given to the costs that are directly involved in the making of a product for a manufacturer or the provision of the service for a service provider.

Gross profit margin

Expressing gross profit as a percentage of price, or revenue, allows comparisons to be made between products and business in similar sectors.

To calculate the **gross profit margin**, use the following formula:

$$\text{Gross profit margin} = \frac{\text{gross profit}}{\text{total sales revenue}} \times 100$$

Superdry's 61.5 per cent gross profit margin in 2016 was far higher than French Connection's 46.3 per cent for the same year. The table below also shows figures for Ted Baker and should help you to see how the gross profit margin is calculated.

> **Gross profit margin**: expresses gross profit as a percentage of sales revenue (or, for an individual item, gross profit as a percentage of the selling price).

	Supergroup plc (Superdry) Year end 30/04/16	Ted Baker plc (Ted Baker clothing) Year end 30/01/16	French Connection plc (French Connection) Year end 31/01/16
Sales revenue	£598 million	£470 million	£164 million
minus **cost of sales**	£230 million	£183 million	£88 million
equals **gross profit**	£368 million	£287 million	£76 million
Gross profit margin	$\frac{£368 \text{ million}}{£598 \text{ million}} \times 100 = \mathbf{61.5\%}$	$\frac{£287 \text{ million}}{£470 \text{ million}} \times 100 = \mathbf{61.1\%}$	$\frac{£76 \text{ million}}{£164 \text{ million}} \times 100 = \mathbf{46.3\%}$

For a business to improve their gross profit margin, they only have two options:

1 Increase the price
2 Cut the cost of buying/making the product

Increasing the price is only sensible if the product's brand is strong enough to retain most customers at a higher price level.

Cutting the cost of buying products could involve:
- negotiating a cheaper price from current suppliers
- setting up a bidding war between suppliers, encouraging them to undercut one another
- redesigning the item to make it easier (and cheaper) to make or use cheaper materials.

Net profit

REVISED

After taking away the running costs of the business from any gross profit, **net profit** is what is left. These running costs may include managers' salaries, marketing expenses, the cost of administration or bills associated with head office. Net profit is the best measure of how well a business has traded for a time period.

> **Net profit**: overall profit made by the business: what is left of gross profit after deducting the running costs or expenses of the business: net profit = gross profit – expenses.

Net profit margin

REVISED

Expressing net profit as a percentage of sales revenue again provides a useful figure for comparisons.

To calculate the net profit margin, use the following formula:

$$\text{Net profit margin} = \frac{\text{net profit}}{\text{total sales revenue}} \times 100$$

The higher the **net profit margin** the better.

> **Net profit margin**: expresses net profit as a percentage of sales revenue (or, for an individual item, net profit as a percentage of the selling price).

The table below shows net profit margin figures for the three clothing chains; clearly French Connection is hugely underperforming compared to the others.

	Supergroup plc (Superdry) Year end 30/04/16	Ted Baker plc (Ted Baker clothing) Year end 30/01/16	French Connection plc (French Connection) Year end 31/01/16
Gross profit	£368 million	£287 million	£76 million
minus **fixed running costs**	£296 million	£228 million	£81 million
equals **net profit**	£72 million	£59 million	−£5 million
Net profit margin	$\frac{£72 \text{ million}}{£598 \text{ million}} \times 100 = \mathbf{12.0\%}$	$\frac{£59 \text{ million}}{£470 \text{ million}} \times 100 = \mathbf{12.6\%}$	$\frac{−£5 \text{ million}}{£164 \text{ million}} \times 100 = \mathbf{−3.0\%}$

Improving net profit margin relies on one of two things:
- improving gross profit
- reducing fixed running costs.

Methods of reducing fixed costs could include:
- changing location to somewhere cheaper
- cutting back on any ineffective promotional activity
- reducing the number of managers
- cutting back on management salaries or bonuses.

Average rate of return

REVISED

Senior managers within a business will regularly make decisions on how to spend large sums of cash in a way to help boost business profit. Investment (spending money now in the hope of a future return) decisions can be aided by the use of **average rate of return (ARR)**.

ARR is a calculation of the average yearly profit on an investment as a percentage of the **sum invested**. Calculating ARR allows comparisons to be made between different proposed investments or even between an investment and the rate of interest the firm would receive by just keeping the sum invested in the bank.

> **Average rate of return (ARR)**: expresses average yearly profit as a percentage of the sum invested. This shows profitability and can be compared with interest rates available on bank deposits.
>
> **Sum invested**: the cash put at risk when investing in new equipment or a new product.

Investment data will usually be presented in a table such as the one below, detailing:
- the initial outlay
- an estimate of yearly profit
- an accumulated profit figure – a running total of the net value of the investment.

Time period	Yearly profit	Accumulated profit
Now: the initial investment	−£80,000	−£80,000
Year 1	+£10,000	−£70,000
Year 2	+£35,000	−£35,000
Year 3	+£45,000	+£10,000
Year 4	+£38,000	+£48,000

To calculate the ARR, follow these steps:

1 Identify the total lifetime profit of the investment (don't forget to deduct the amount initially invested from any returns).

2 Calculate the average profit per year, by dividing lifetime profit by the years the investment is expected to last.

3 Apply the ARR formula: $\text{ARR} = \dfrac{\text{average yearly profit}}{\text{initial investment}} \times 100$

So, for the previous table:

1 Lifetime profit = £48,000

2 Yearly profit = £48,000 / 4 = £12,000

3 ARR = (£12,000 / £80,000) × 100 = 15% per year

This figure can then be compared to ARRs for other possible uses of the £80,000 or the interest rate the firm would receive if they kept the £80,000 in the bank. The simple rule is, the higher, the better.

Now test yourself

TESTED

1 Use the information in the table below to calculate gross profit margin and net profit margin for Company X and Company Y.

	Company X	Company Y
Sales revenue	£25 million	£40 million
minus **cost of sales**	£10 million	£20 million
equals **gross profit**	£15 million	£20 million
minus **fixed running costs**	£10 million	£15 million
equals **net profit**	£5 million	£5 million

2 Explain which company is doing better and why.

3 Use the information in the table below to calculate ARR for the investment project.

Time period	Yearly profit	Accumulated profit
NOW: the initial investment	−£150,000	−£150,000
Year 1	+£25,000	−£125,000
Year 2	+£50,000	−£75,000
Year 3	+£75,000	0
Year 4	+£100,000	+£100,000
Year 5	+£100,000	+£200,000

Answers on page 107

2.4.2 Understanding business performance

Use and interpretation of business data

Given how much quantitative data is generated by businesses, the ability to interpret and understand data on business performance is a crucial skill for managers and business students. Data can come from different areas of a business and can be used to help to support, inform and justify key business decisions.

Information from graphs and charts

The commonest types of visual representation of data are:
- line graphs
- bar charts
- pie charts.

Each way of showing data has its strengths and weaknesses, as summarised in the table below.

	Line graphs	Bar charts	Pie charts
Advantages	Good for data shown over many time periods ... and for looking at how one factor affects another, e.g. sales in pounds and money spent on advertising	Good for data shown over two or three time periods Good for comparing the size of several different items, e.g. populations of the ten biggest countries	Good for showing proportions, e.g. Cadbury's share of the UK chocolate market Size of the circle can be made proportional to the quantity it represents
Disadvantages	Too many lines can be confusing, so it can only be used to compare two or three series of data A risk of oversimplifying in assuming that an upward line will stay upward in the future	Cannot easily be used to compare data over many time periods If there is too much data it gets confusing to the eye	Pies show big differences clearly, but for small differences a bar chart can be clearer Cannot show trends over a number of years

Typical mistake

As the table shows, different graphs and charts are more suited to showing different types of data so think carefully about what you are trying to show before deciding on the best way to present data.

Line graph: shows data presented as lines, making it easy to identify trends, especially if time is on the horizontal axis.

Bar chart: shows data presented so that the height of the bar represents the quantity involved; it is good for making comparisons.

Pie chart: shows data presented in a circle, with each slice of the pie representing a proportion of the whole; it is good for proportions of a total – for example, market share.

Financial data

Key pieces of financial data that are used to help make decisions have been dealt with separately already:

- gross profit margin
- net profit margin
- average rate of return (ARR)
- profit or loss on any individual deal
- break-even point
- cash flows.

Marketing data

Analysis of a company's own sales figures can provide valuable insight. In addition to sales figures, market research data about customer attitudes to the firm's products or services can make things even clearer. This may come from secondary or primary sources.

Market data

Analysis of data on total market size, changes in market size (growth or shrinkage) or figures for different segments within a market can provide crucial insights on what markets to enter or leave, to prioritise where promotional money is spent or to decide where to invest funds in developing new products.

The use and limitations of financial data

REVISED

Key questions for managers to ask when assessing how well their business is performing include:

- What are the current trends in market share?
- What are the current trends in profit?
- What are the current trends in cash balances?

The trick to understanding performance is to really try to evaluate what the data shows. Managers should ask why the trends they identify are happening and must keep an open mind to the causes of these trends; the data might, for example, show the effects of mistakes made by the manager. It is important that the manager accepts what the data is telling them, rather than settling on some other cause (that is not their fault).

This last point hints at one of the limitations of using financial data to make business decisions. Managers can consciously or subconsciously introduce bias into their interpretation of data or even data that they generate themselves.

A further issue with using financial or other figure-based data is the misguided belief that numbers must represent facts. Asking where the numbers have come from is vital when looking at such data; some may be factual, but other data may be based only on estimates and guesses.

> **Exam tip**
>
> Always try to spot the source of information provided and then judge how reliable that source is likely to be.

Now test yourself

TESTED

1 What type of chart or table is best at showing trends over time?
2 What type of chart or table is best at showing proportions, such as market share of different firms in a market?
3 Briefly explain two reasons why managers may make poor decisions using financial data.

Answers on page 108

Summary

Key measures of financial success for a business are:
- gross profit margin
- net profit margin.

To assess an investment, calculate average rate of return (ARR).

For all three financial measures, higher numbers are better.

To improve gross profit margin:
- increase selling price
- decrease cost of making/buying the product.

To improve net profit margin:
- improve gross profit
- decrease fixed running costs.

Common forms of graph or chart are:
- line graphs
- bar charts
- pie charts.

Line graphs are good for showing trends in data.

Bar charts are good for comparing the size of several different items.

Pie charts are good for showing proportions of a whole.

Other financial data used includes:
- profit or loss on a specific deal
- break-even point
- cash flow balances.

Other common quantitative data used in business includes:
- marketing data
- market data.

Exam practice

XYZ plc has just announced financial results for last year. The pie chart shows where their £200m revenue went.

The company has £40m to invest in a new project, but will only do so if the annual rate of return generated is over 12 per cent. The project is expected to generate the following annual profits.

Time period	Annual profit
Now	–£40m
Year 1	+£15m
Year 2	+£15m
Year 3	+£34m

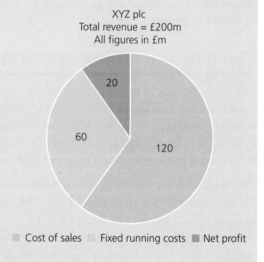

XYZ plc
Total revenue = £200m
All figures in £m

20
60
120

■ Cost of sales   Fixed running costs   ■ Net profit

1 Calculate:
   a) gross profit   (2)
   b) gross profit margin   (2)
   c) net profit margin   (2)
   for XYZ plc for last year.
2 Justify whether XYZ plc's new project beat the target ARR of 12 per cent. (9)
3 Which type of graph or chart would be best to use to show directors the trend in XYZ plc's sales revenue total over the past ten years? (1)
4 Which type of graph or chart would be best to use to show gross and net profit margin figures over the past three years? (1)

Answers on page 111

ONLINE

Topic 2.5 Making human resources decisions

2.5.1 Organisational structures

Structure refers to the different levels of formal power within an organisation. Most organisations will identify who is in charge of whom and therefore who should be answerable to whom. This helps to ensure that:

- everyone knows where to go for help
- everybody understands who their boss is
- all bosses understand who they are responsible for
- communication flows through the organisation are clear.

Power and pay will be greater higher up the organisation, with those further up the **organisation chart** taking greater responsibilities and being rewarded for this.

> **Organisation chart**: a diagram that shows the internal structure of an organisation.

Hierarchical and flat structures

REVISED

Hierarchy refers to formal levels of responsibility and authority in an organisation. Larger organisations tend to have more layers, forming a pyramid-shaped structure. In these tall, **hierarchical structures**, one manager will be responsible for only a handful of people.

Advantages of these tall structures are:
- Promotion opportunities should be regular.
- It is easy to maintain standards with clear lines of accountability.
- It is easier to check people's work with managers and supervisors overseeing just a few people each.

Disadvantages include:
- With clear levels, position becomes a status symbol and can create a divide between managers and workers.
- It is hard for the person at the top to communicate with people at the bottom as there are so many layers for messages to pass through.
- Too many layers of management can slow down decision making.

The alternative is a **flatter structure**. This is made possible by increasing the number of people that each manager is in charge of, meaning fewer managers are needed, and fewer layers. People at lower layers will have more responsibility than in a hierarchical tall structure.

Benefits of a flat structure include:
- Fewer managers means money is saved on salaries.
- Managers give more responsibility to workers.
- This extra responsibility can increase job satisfaction.
- There is faster and more efficient communication between managers and staff.

But disadvantages can include:
- Each manager has a heavier workload with more people to oversee.
- Managers have to rely on junior staff to work safely with less supervision.
- Managers may lose control over subordinates.
- This can lead to overwork and stress.
- There are fewer opportunities for promotion.

> **Hierarchical structure**: an organisation with many layers of management, therefore creating a tall organisational pyramid.
>
> **Flat structure**: an organisation with few layers of hierarchy, presumably because each manager is responsible for many staff.

> **Exam tip**
>
> When assessing organisational structure, consider the type of worker and how much supervision they are likely to need. Skilled, experienced staff will need less supervision, so a flatter structure works well, but unskilled inexperienced staff may need to be watched more closely, meaning a hierarchical structure works best.

Centralised and decentralised organisations

Another way to classify organisational structure is by referring to where most decision making takes place. In some businesses, all major decisions are made at head office and then all branches of the business must follow the plan laid down by head office. These are **centralised organisations**: decision-making power is centralised at head office. Benefits and drawbacks of centralised organisations are shown in the table below.

Centralised organisation: an organisation in which most decisions are made at head office.

Benefits	Drawbacks
Decisions can be taken with an overview of the whole business	There is less delegation, so the company may be slow to respond to local changes
Encourages consistency within the organisation	If local staff are not allowed to make changes, opportunities may be lost
Decision making can be quick, with no need to consult other levels of the structure	Lack of involvement may reduce job satisfaction for local managers

The alternative is to **decentralise** decision making, allowing local managers to make decisions that suit local conditions. Although this can lead to some inconsistencies within the organisation, clear benefits include better local decision making and increased motivation for local staff.

Decentralised organisation: an organisation that allows staff to make decisions at a local level.

Effective communication

Communication in a business is necessary in order to:
- provide and collect information about the business
- give instructions
- ensure all workers are working towards the same goal.

Effective communication has several common features:
- clear and easily understood
- accurate
- complete
- appropriate
- via the right medium
- with a chance for feedback.

Poor communication may be the result of weaknesses in the key features shown above. However, other major causes of ineffective communication may be too much or too little communication.

Consequences of **insufficient communication**:
- misunderstandings and rumours
- inefficiency with a lack of sharing of ideas and solutions
- low levels of motivation
- lost profits.

Consequences of **excessive communication**, most often email:
- information overload
- people spending too much time reading emails and not enough time doing things
- important emails missed in the barrage of email received daily
- demotivated staff struggling to cope.

Communication: the passing of information from one person or organisation to another.

Insufficient communication: too little communication, which might leave some staff under-informed and demotivated.

Excessive communication: too much communication, causing overload for staff; a particular problem with email.

Typical mistake

Excessive communication is a great example of how technology can make communication worse: do not assume that technology only improves communication.

Barriers to effective communication

Common **barriers to effective communication** include:

- The person sending the communication may not explain themselves properly.
- The receiver may not understand the message due to technical language or 'jargon'.
- The receiver may not hear or receive the message due to a technical problem.
- The message may be distorted in transmission.
- The failure to provide the opportunity for feedback (which could overcome many of these problems).

> **Barrier to communication**: something that prevents the flow of communication.

Different ways of working

REVISED

The three broad categories of employment in the UK are:

- **Full time** – usually between 35 and 40 hours per week.
- **Part-time** – less than 35 hours and usually predictable days/hours.
- **Flexible hours** – where hours/days can vary from week to week and there is no guaranteed number of hours to work per week. Zero hours contracts fit into this category, so called because employees are not guaranteed any work.

In addition, millions of people in the UK are self-employed. This may not be the entrepreneurial image we have of self-employment as these may be relatively low paid roles such as cleaners, care workers and taxi drivers who may be forced to be self-employed with companies not wishing to take on responsibilities for sick or holiday pay.

Employees are not self-employed, that is to say, those who have a contract with the business they are employed by (whether full-time or part-time) are likely to have been offered one of three different types of contract.

Permanent contracts

You are employed indefinitely and the contract is open-ended. Permanent contracts offer:

- stable earnings
- job security
- regular contributions to your pension
- usually sick pay
- being valued by an employer as worth training.

Temporary contracts

These contracts run out after a set period of time, perhaps six months or a year. They will often be offered to newly qualified staff, in case they are not up to the job and so need not have their contract renewed. They offer:

- flexibility for a worker to take time out of their career for travelling or other purposes
- the chance to try several different types of job and employer.

Freelance contracts

These are usually incredibly short-term contracts (perhaps a day or a week) where an employee is contracted to work on one particular project and then released.

Impact of technology on how we work

Fast broadband, smartphones, Wi-Fi and video chat applications all mean that it is possible to work with others without being beside them.

Technology and efficiency

Yes, technology can increase efficiency, with technological developments meaning that some tasks can be automated and done faster or more accurately than a human can do them. Technology can also be used as a tool for monitoring and controlling staff, with people working in giant e-commerce warehouses, picking stock to be dispatched, told what to do, in how many seconds, all day, by their own handheld devices.

Exam tip

This is another opportunity to build an argument showing how improved efficiency can generate more output with similar fixed costs, which means cost per unit is lower, which allows the business to cut its selling price and make the same profit or make a higher gross profit margin.

Technology and remote working

Working from a location other than the office, such as from home or while you travel, is known as remote working. Although this type of working is now made possible due to communication technology, the practice can lead to a lack of face-to-face interaction between colleagues, leading to feelings of isolation and denying opportunities for chance conversations at work to generate new ideas.

Now test yourself

TESTED

1 State two benefits of a tall organisational structure.
2 State two benefits of a decentralised organisational structure.
3 List three possible problems caused by insufficient communication.

Answers on page 108

2.5.2 Effective recruitment

Once a business grows to be bigger than the entrepreneur can manage themselves, they will need to recruit staff to fulfil the jobs that need doing. A range of different positions will need to be covered in a large business, detailed below.

Different job roles and responsibilities

REVISED

- **Directors** – Members of the board of directors are the people who make the biggest decisions faced by the business. They will decide on recruiting senior managers, and the aims and objectives for the business, as well as discuss major issues such as which markets to sell to.
- **Senior managers** – Any manager's job is to organise others to carry out tasks. Senior managers will decide what needs to be done, then decide on the right middle-manager to handle this, ensuring that a task gets done effectively.
- **Supervisors/team leaders** – The role of these junior managers is to ensure that the staff below them do what they are supposed to do.
- **Operational and support staff** – Operational refers to whether a member of staff has specific responsibility for meeting a target set by the business that is focused on achieving the business's aims or objectives. The role of support staff is to help operational staff, providing assistance with computer networks, facilities and buildings maintenance, cleaning and even catering.

How businesses recruit people

REVISED

Choosing which people to hire means getting to know as much about them as a potential worker as possible, then trying to figure out if they are the right person for the job that needs doing. Several documents will be used in this process.

Documents

Initially, the business will draw up a **job description** and a **person specification**, so they can be clear on what job needs doing and what skills and experience the ideal candidate might have. These will be used to help choose which applicant is right for the job: finding the one who best fits the person specification.

People applying for the job will complete and submit an **application form**, a **CV** and **references**. These three main documents will help the business to understand what the applicants are like. Using the information provided by these documents, possibly followed up by an interview, managers will decide who best fits the person specification.

> **Job description**: a short account of the main features of the job.
>
> **Person specification**: a description of the type of person who would best fit the job: their character, their experience and skills.
>
> **Application form**: a series of questions a job-seeker must fill in when trying to get an employer interested in interviewing them.
>
> **CV (curriculum vitae)**: sets out the person's qualifications, experience and any other relevant facts (it literally means 'story of life').
>
> **References**: people such as teachers or previous bosses who are willing to answer questions about the qualities of a job applicant.

Recruitment methods

A business faces two basic options when it needs to fill a vacancy: promote or redeploy somebody already working for the business – internal recruitment; or hire somebody new to the business – external recruitment. Both options have strengths and weaknesses, detailed in the tables below.

Advantages of internal recruitment	Disadvantages of internal recruitment
It is likely to be quicker and cheaper than external recruitment.	Existing workers may not have the skills required, especially if the business wants to develop new products or markets.
Greater variety of promotion opportunities may motivate employees.	Relying on existing employees may lead to a stagnation of ideas and approaches within the business.
The firm will already be aware of the employee's skills and attitude to work.	Recruiting internally will create a vacancy elsewhere.

Advantages of external recruitment	Disadvantages of external recruitment
It should result in a wider range of candidates than internal recruitment.	It can be an expensive and time-consuming process, using up valuable resources.
Candidates may already have the skills required to carry out the job in question, avoiding the need for (and cost of) training.	It can have a demotivating effect on members of the existing workforce, who may have missed out on promotion.

If the business chooses to use external recruitment, it will need to find a way to tell potential applicants that the job is available. The most common methods for doing this are:

- media advertising – producing an advert to be displayed in newspapers, specialist magazines, employment websites or even TV
- job centres – government-run organisations that help people to find work
- commercial recruitment agencies – firms that exist to handle recruiting staff for other firms, in return for a fee
- website – a company may advertise vacancies on their own website.

Now test yourself

1 What name is given to the most senior staff in a business?
2 Which two documents does a business use to start the recruitment process?
3 Why is internal recruitment less likely to be suitable when recruiting extra staff while a business grows in size?

Answers on page 108

2.5.3 Effective training and development

Training helps a business's employees to gain new skills or develop existing skills. The fundamental benefit to a business of providing training is that jobs are done more efficiently, faster and more accurately.

The table below shows the benefits and costs to companies of providing training.

Benefits	Costs
Improving employees' skills should improve efficiency and quality.	Paying to send staff on courses or paying internal trainers to train staff will carry a financial cost.
A wider range of skills available in a business allows them to respond to changes in the market more quickly.	The normal production or operations of the business may be disrupted while training is taking place.
Training is likely to boost the motivation of staff by giving them opportunities for development and promotion.	Developing a highly skilled workforce may make them attractive to other businesses that try to persuade them to change jobs, allowing another business to benefit from training provided.

How businesses train and develop employees

REVISED

Formal and informal training

The planned or **formal training** provided by a business tends to be what most people mean when discussing training and development. However, many employees discover that the unplanned snippets of advice from more experienced co-workers help them improve their efficiency far more. A supervisor's role in offering this **informal training** can have a huge impact on the efficiency of their team.

> **Typical mistake**
>
> Formal training does not need to happen in a classroom. A plan to improve managers' problem solving skills through an outdoor adventure course is still formal, planned training.

Self-learning

The process of learning from mistakes – **self-learning** – lies at the heart of most training. As your studies have probably shown you, making a mistake and understanding why it was a mistake will really help you to understand the right way to do things as long as you learn from your mistakes and do not repeat the same error time and time again.

Ongoing training for all employees

Too many companies train staff when they begin a job and then offer no further training, unless perhaps a new piece of technology is introduced. The most successful training programmes ensure regular opportunities are provided for all staff, giving them a sense of continually developing their skills. Without **ongoing training**, employees may leave the business as they feel they are not making progress at work.

> **Formal training**: the official training programme – for example, a two-year graduate training programme.
>
> **Informal training**: the unexpected, unplanned extra advice or demonstrations that come from colleagues or occasionally customers.
>
> **Self-learning**: teaching yourself, perhaps by thinking why a problem occurred and making sure you learn from your mistakes.
>
> **Ongoing training**: regular, perhaps weekly training sessions for all staff.

Use of target-setting and performance reviews

Especially in larger businesses, a formal system for trying to ensure staff development involves regular **target-setting** for staff. Then, after a period of time, a **performance review** meeting with a manager allows staff to discuss whether or not they met the targets and how they could have done even better. This can identify training needs. In addition, the process can really reinforce to staff how they are developing.

Why businesses train and develop employees

The two main reasons why businesses invest in training staff are subtly different. Retraining staff to use new technology that is introduced is common sense: staff need to know how to do their job: if the job changes, they need retraining. Many businesses also realise that training has a subtle effect on employees' emotions. Feeling valued and feeling a sense of personal growth can boost motivation and loyalty.

> **Target-setting**: when you are set goals by a manager and your job is to achieve them.
>
> **Performance reviews**: discussion between you and your boss (perhaps every six months) about how well you are doing against the targets set for you.
>
> **Retention**: a calculation of how many staff stay loyal rather than leaving – for example, staff staying as a percentage of all staff.

> **Typical mistake**
>
> Studying GCSE Business means you will be looking at issues from the perspective of a business. Check carefully if you find yourself explaining the benefits of training to an employee: questions are far more likely to focus on the benefits to the business of training staff.

Motivation and retention

Training is used by many businesses to help motivate staff. This works in two main ways.
- Staff feel valued as their employer is willing to spend money on them to boost their skills.
- Staff feel a sense of personal growth, a sort of pride that they can now do more than they could before.

Both of these effects tend to lead to committed staff, engaged in their work, who are more productive and loyal to the business. This loyalty means that staff are less likely to leave for other jobs, which boosts staff **retention** and lowers the costs the business faces when needing to recruit replacement staff.

Training ➡ Motivation ➡ Retention

Training helps to motivate and retain staff

Retraining to use new technology

For a business introducing any new way of doing things, especially a new piece of technology, their investment is wasted if the technology is not used properly. Therefore, the introduction of technology should be accompanied by training for the staff who will use it. This technical instruction should form part of a planned training programme.

> **Exam tip**
>
> Examiners want to see you explain why one thing leads to another. Linking training to improved motivation and then linking that to better retention demonstrates excellent analysis within your answer.

Now test yourself

1 Briefly explain the difference between formal and informal training.
2 How does regular training help to improve motivation?
3 Why should regular training reduce the costs of producing a product?

Answers on page 108

2.5.4 Motivation

The importance of motivation

REVISED

Having staff who want to work, want to do the best job possible and are committed to the success of the business offers many advantages, including:

- higher productivity
- attracting the best employees
- lower staff turnover (retaining employees), so lower recruitment costs
- better quality production or service
- more ideas from staff.

The question for businesses is how do they motivate staff in order to gain these benefits? There are two broad approaches to motivating staff, though many accept that a range of methods is needed. Some managers believe that financial methods of motivation work best, while others believe that non-financial methods of motivation work more effectively at creating a real will to work rather than simply doing enough to get paid.

The basic reason why motivation matters so much to business is illustrated below.

Motivation is vital to business success

Financial methods of motivation

REVISED

Remuneration

Most jobs (excluding volunteers) involve receiving payment in return for your time. This pay may be per hour worked or, commonly for those in full-time permanent jobs, a salary. For those paid a salary, their monthly pay is unrelated to how much effort they have put in. For workers in the private sector (working for privately owned businesses), they may also receive **fringe benefits**, sometimes called perks, such as the use of a company phone, a subsidised canteen or leisure facilities. These methods of **remuneration** are all based on the assumption that pay does not motivate, but employees must be financially rewarded so they can afford to live. For those who believe that 'money motivates', there are systems that offer financial rewards based on how hard or how well you work.

> **Exam tip**
>
> Don't forget that financial methods of motivation will cost the business directly; to be worthwhile, they must generate more extra revenue or costs savings than it costs to implement pay, bonuses or commission.

> **Remuneration**: all the financial rewards received from work, whether direct, such as a salary, or indirect, such as free membership of a sports club.
>
> **Fringe benefits**: rewards you get from work other than pay, such as a company phone or car.

Bonuses

Bonuses are extra payments over and above your basic wage or salary. They can be used to reward top performers and will usually be linked to a target, which can either be personal or a target for the whole business (in which case all the staff would share a bonus pot). The benefits and drawbacks of bonuses are shown in the table below.

Benefits	Drawbacks
An unpromised bonus might be a great reward for a worker who has achieved great things during the year.	A bonus-driven business pushes staff to lower their standards in pursuit of the money (the bankers' bonus problem).
If a company has made huge profits, staff would be thrilled to receive a payout.	Firms can end up giving bonuses for staff completing ordinary tasks, such as footballers being paid 'appearance money'.
Bonuses may be a help in getting staff to do the less pleasant parts of their jobs, e.g. a bonus for getting dull paperwork tasks done on time.	Once staff get used to bonuses, they can come to expect them rather than be thrilled by them. The 10 per cent bonus at John Lewis in 2016 was actually down sharply on the 17 per cent in 2013.

Commission

For people whose job involves sales, one way of offering a financial reward is to pay them a **commission** on everything they sell. This should be in addition to a basic wage, though some companies will only pay commission to sales staff.

> **Commission**: being paid a percentage of the value of a sale you have made – for example, a 10 per cent commission.

Promotion

Being given a more important job in the organisational structure is usually the route to building a successful career. The table below shows how promotion should work in a business and contrasts this with how it actually works in some businesses, meaning that striving for a promotion may not be an effective method of motivating staff.

Promotion: the way it should be	Promotion: the way it often is	Promotion: making it better
Promotions go to the best, the brightest or those showing leadership potential.	Promotions go to those whose face fits and who agree with management policies.	Managers should learn that different viewpoints can lead to better decisions.
Juniors showing leadership potential should get equal training for equal opportunity.	Ethnic minority staff don't get put on the training courses that fit with a promotion push.	Companies should check whether training opportunities are provided equally.
Staff should all aspire to get promoted and therefore have the incentive to be their best.	Seeing how things are, many staff don't look for promotion; they look to get out.	If not many are applying for promotion, senior managers should investigate why.

Non-financial methods of motivation

Job rotation

Carrying out the same task day in day out will get boring for most (unless the task is fascinating and varied). As a result, some businesses will use **job rotation**, allowing workers to switch between different tasks as a way of preventing the boredom that comes with monotonous work.

Job enrichment

Designing a job that offers staff the opportunity to take on new challenges and more responsible tasks may be a better way of motivating staff than job rotation. An **enriched job** is likely to include:

● a complete unit of work – seeing something through from start to finish
● self-checking – nobody else will check the quality of your work
● direct feedback – you can tell how well you are doing without needing someone else to come in and judge.

Autonomy

Giving staff the chance to decide what they will do at work and how they will do it can be a huge motivator. However, it presents clear issues if you cannot trust your staff. This is just the type of dilemma that makes running a business so hard.

Job rotation: having several tasks to do at work to relieve the boredom of doing the same thing all the time.

Job enrichment: being given a range of activities and responsibilities that enable the worker to learn and grow.

Autonomy: the independent power to decide what you are going to do at work.

Typical mistake

Don't confuse job rotation – doing several tasks with the same level of challenge, with job enrichment – doing several tasks with increasing levels of challenge and responsibility.

Now test yourself

1 List three benefits of a motivated workforce.
2 State two payment methods based on the belief that people work harder to get more money.
3 Briefly explain the difference between job rotation and job enrichment.

Answers on page 108

Summary

Organisational structures can be hierarchical (tall) or flat depending on the number of different levels.

A structure is centralised or decentralised according to where decisions are made, either at head office (centralised) or at a local level (decentralised).

Communication in a business is necessary in order to:
- provide and collect information about the business
- give instructions
- ensure all workers are working towards the same goal.

Effective communication has several common features:
- clear and easily understood
- accurate
- complete
- appropriate
- via the right medium
- with a chance for feedback.

Consequences of insufficient communication:
- misunderstandings and rumours
- inefficiency with a lack of sharing of ideas and solutions
- low levels of motivation
- lost profits.

Consequences of excessive communication, most often email:
- information overload
- people spend too much time reading emails and not enough time doing things
- important emails may get missed in the barrage of email received daily
- demotivated staff struggling to cope.

Common barriers to effective communication include:
- the person sending the communication may not explain themselves properly
- the receiver may not understand the message due to technical language or 'jargon'
- the receiver may not hear or receive the message due to a technical problem
- the message may be distorted in transmission
- failure to provide the opportunity for feedback (which could overcome many of these problems).

The three broad categories of employment in the UK are:
- full-time
- part-time
- flexible hours.

Contracts can be:
- permanent
- temporary
- freelance.

The two major impacts of technology on how people work relate to:
- efficiency
- remote working.

Different managerial roles, in descending order of power, include:
- director
- senior manager
- supervisor/team leader.

Documents used in the recruitment process include:
- job description
- person specification
- application form
- CV (curriculum vitae)
- references.

When recruiting, businesses face a choice of using internal or external recruitment.

Benefits of training staff include:
- improved efficiency
- improved quality
- better ability to respond to changes in the market
- improved retention of staff
- improved motivation.

Methods of training staff include:
- formal and informal training
- self-learning
- ongoing training for all employees
- target-setting and performance reviews.

Training may need to be provided to help staff use new technology.

A motivated workforce brings a number of benefits to a business, including:
- higher productivity
- lower staff turnover, so lower recruitment costs
- better quality levels
- more ideas from staff.

Financial methods of motivation include:
- remuneration (including fringe benefits)
- bonuses
- commission
- promotion.

Non-financial methods include:
- job rotation
- job enrichment
- autonomy.

Now test yourself and Exam practice answers can be found on page 104 onwards

Exam practice

SoozeApps is a producer of app-based games, based in London, with a remarkable record of success in its brief history. Founded just five years ago, the company now employs 30 staff, developing a range of apps, all designed to fit in with the company's aim of only producing genuinely innovative apps, unlike any other on the market.

With growth has come the need to cope with managing a larger organisation. The company has kept a flat structure, with just three levels. Staff work in two departments: the app developers, and the support staff who handle finance, marketing and administrative functions.

The company pays all staff a generous salary and offers fringe benefits, including a company phone and free hot and cold soft drinks in the office. Keeping staff skills topped up depends on substantial investment in training, so all staff spend a minimum of 15 days a year engaged in training activities, provided by the company.

1 Outline what is meant by fringe benefits. (2)
2 Outline two reasons why the business may have decided to use a flat structure. (4)
3 SoozeApps needs to replace their head app developer, who has just left to become a teacher. Justify whether they should use internal or external recruitment to fill the vacancy. (9)

Answers on page 111

ONLINE

Now test yourself answers

1.1.1

1 Technological change; changes in what consumers want; products or services becoming obsolete.
2 Probably a mobile phone or games console.
3 They are based on already successful ideas, proven to be popular with customers.
4 A diverse workforce, enough profit reinvested in new ideas and motivated staff.

1.1.2

1 Business failure; financial loss; lack of security.
2 Business success; profit and wealth; independence.
3 Risk comes from uncertainty. As businesses cannot predict the future and are affected by external factors – beyond their control – all must face and manage risk.

1.1.3

1 Convenience; branding; quality; design; USP.
2 Financial resources; human resources (chefs, waiters); physical resources (food, cookers, tables, cutlery).
3 Produce goods and services; meet customer needs; add value.

1.2.1

1 Price; quality; choice; convenience; being efficient and reliable; design.
2 a) Design and either quality or reliability.
   b) Price and either design or reliability.
   c) Convenience and reliability.

1.2.2

1 Questionnaires; surveys; observations; online ratings.
2 As each focus group involves one skilled researcher who will be well paid and only a handful of respondents, the cost per person involved is high, especially as each focus group discussion may last several hours.
3 To identify and understand customer needs; to identify gaps in the market; to reduce risk; to inform business decisions.

1.2.3

1 Splitting up customers into different groups, where members of each segment have similar needs, helps a business to meet those needs more precisely, by adapting the product to suit that particular type of customer.
2 Location; income; lifestyle; age; gender; race; religion.
3 If you can give a customer 'exactly what they are looking for', i.e. a product that meets their needs precisely, they will often pay more than they would for a product that 'sort of does what I want'.
4 Age (young to old) and price (high to low) would be sensible choices. Perhaps more interesting may be to show purpose on one axis (from high performance to casual streetwear). This could be plotted against age.

1.2.4

1 The cost of a great location will be very high.
2 This identifies ways they can be beaten.
3 This may harm the company's reputation, making it hard to increase their price later.

1.3.1

1 Targets allow a clear judgement on whether the business is succeeding or whether things need changing.
2 Survival; profit; sales; market share; financial security.
3 Social objectives; personal satisfaction; challenge; independence; control.

1.3.2

1 £10,000 − £8,000 = £2,000 profit.
2 Total costs are £8,000 when 1,000 units are sold. If fixed costs are £5,000, the other £3,000 of costs must be variable. Divide by 1,000 units to see that variable costs per unit are £3.
3 a) Selling price = £450 (£90,000/200).
   b) Fixed costs = £18,000.

1.3.3

1 At start-up and during spells of rapid growth.
2 Cash flow forecasting; negotiating an overdraft; keeping the cash coming in; reducing cash outflows.
3 Net cash flow is minus £100 (usually shown as (£100), with the brackets indicating a minus figure), so closing balance falls to £100.

1.3.4

1 Bank overdraft and trade credit.
2 To start up the business; to finance the purchase of assets with a long life, such as property and buildings; to provide the money needed for expansion; to build a bigger factory or buy another business.
3 Interest payments on the loan; repaying the amount actually borrowed.

1.4.1

1 These businesses may build up debts, meaning the owner will want to limit the amount they personally can lose.
2 Sole trader; partnership.
3 Losing up to 8 per cent of revenue immediately as a royalty payment may mean there is less money left after costs are deducted.

1.4.2

1 Proximity to market; proximity to materials; proximity to labour; proximity to competitors.
2 Proximity to market.
3 With no way for customers to buy their goods online, they must be easily accessible to as many customers as possible.

1.4.3

1 Product; price; promotion; place.
2 A clear image (that is different to any rival product).
3 Changes may be needed to cope with competitors' actions; changing consumer tastes; changes in technology.

1.4.4

1 To raise finance.
2 Business idea; business aims and objectives; target market; marketing plan; forecast revenue, costs and profit; cash flow forecast; sources of finance; location; marketing mix.
3 Confusing the plan with reality; may prevent flexibility; too little time spent on people.

1.5.1

1 Shareholders will want the store to open and be busy to maximise revenue and therefore profit. However, the local community may fight the store opening as it will add to traffic problems.
2 Being paid a fair price; being paid on time.
3 Customers may want long opening hours, while the local community may want peace and quiet in the evenings.

1.5.2

1 Promotion.
2 Many people buy using e-commerce; apps allow easy organisation of delivery.
3 By using the internet to research cheaper suppliers.

1.5.3

1 Consumer Rights Act (2015); Trade Descriptions Act (1968).
2 Recruitment; pay; promotion.
3 Everyone plays by the same rules; legislation can increase businesses' costs.

1.5.4

1 Revenue is likely to fall as fewer consumers will be able to afford a luxury car.
2 Consumers have less money to spend so sales may fall; the cost of any loans the business has will rise.
3 It is easier to export if the pound is weak.

1.5.5

1 The robot should be able to produce more efficiently, reducing the costs of production, leaving more profit.
2 Poundland should see an increase in sales in a downturn, so they may buy extra stock or even open new stores.
3 A weaker pound makes exporting easier so they may need more staff to cater for increased demand from overseas.

2.1.1

1 New products; new markets.
2 Huge growth can occur overnight; greater power in dealing with suppliers and buyers; scope to reduce costs by eliminating duplicated jobs.
3 Retained profits; sale of assets.

2.1.2

1 Focus on survival; exit markets; reduce product range; reduce workforce.
2 Increase workforce; focus on growth; enter new markets.
3 Changes in technology; changes in market conditions; poor performance or arrival of a new boss.

2.1.3

1 More competition from imports; able to sell abroad more easily; may set up production elsewhere in the world.
2 With many cars exported from the UK to other EU countries, import tariffs may be applied once the UK leaves the EU, making those cars more expensive and less attractive to EU drivers.
3 The most likely impact is the need to provide left-hand drive cars instead of cars for the UK market with the steering wheel on the right; air conditioning may need to be fitted to all cars given local temperatures.

2.1.4

1 They are placing profit above the welfare of staff.
2 It may be cheaper; it may provide better protection for the product.
3 Recycling; CO_2 emissions.

2.2.1

1 Aesthetics; cost; function.
2 Introduction; growth; maturity; decline.
3 Find new uses; change appearance; encourage more frequent use; adapt the product.

2.2.2

1 A highly differentiated product can be sold for a higher price.
2 To encourage consumers to try the drink, hoping they will like it and continue to buy once prices rise.
3 Easier price comparison via the web has driven prices down.

2.2.3

1 Rather than the cost of what you give away, the major cost is likely to be paying the people giving the product away.
2 They may well devalue the brand in the eyes of consumers.
3 They are relatively cheap methods of promotion to use. In addition they can be effective at targeting those particularly interested in the product.

2.2.4

1 The traditional channel as so many are sold through small convenience stores.
2 They will receive all of the price paid by consumers, instead of the retailer and the wholesaler taking a cut of that price.
3 Convince retailers the product is different; provide promotional support; make sure the retailer's share of profit is acceptable.

2.2.5

1 Consumers may not be aware the product exists if the promotional activity doesn't reach them; the promotion may give off the wrong image for the product, putting people off buying.

2

Elements of marketing mix	Effects on other Ps	
Product	Cost and features will have major impact on Price	Type of product usually determines the distribution channel (Place)
Price	Price level will determine what type of retailers (Place) will be appropriate	Price will affect the key Promotional messages: classy for high price, value for low price
Promotion	Special offers may focus on short-term cuts to Price	Retailers (Place) will need to be informed of planned promotions to buy more stock
Place	Promotion may need to inform consumers of where to buy the product	If distribution channel involves wholesalers and retailers, this will push up Price paid by consumer

3 Product:
- Features of the product that other companies cannot or do not offer give a competitive edge.
- Variations can help a firm to stand out by better enabling them to meet customers' needs with the right size, flavour or colour.
- Great quality of manufacture, using great materials, is another way that the product can give a competitive advantage.
- Design, as Apple keeps showing us, can give a real edge over rivals.

Price:
- A company that can sell the cheapest product on the market has a competitive advantage.
- Even if there are cheaper similar products, if a company can set the lowest price among its closest rivals, they may be seen as the cheapest in their market niche.

Promotion:
- Brand image can be a major advantage for a business. Despite the massive amount of investment usually needed to build a powerful and popular brand, it may be worth it if the brand is *the* brand that consumers favour above all others.
- Some companies, with the help of their advertising agencies, develop incredibly memorable adverts or advertising campaigns that provide a real competitive advantage.
- A business that harnesses technology better than any rival to understand their customers may be better able to target consumers with the right promotions and offers. This more accurate targeting can represent a genuine competitive advantage.

Place:
- Getting the product into more stores than others, often due to a great team of salespeople or very generous margins offered to retailers, can give a business an edge.
- Having the product stocked in a type of store that business rivals are unable to get into can help a business stand out from their competitors.

- Better online facilities can make a company's website one that online browsers really enjoy or designing a brilliantly functioning app can help to gain a competitive edge.

2.3.1

1 Can lower costs of production; can speed up production.
2 Expensive to set up.
3 Lowers production costs; increases productivity; more consistent quality; possibly reduced flexibility.

2.3.2

1 Buffer (stock).
2 With less stock to store, less space needs to be paid for to store it.
3 Quality; deliveries; availability; cost; trust.

2.3.3

1 Cold food; food tastes bad; poorly presented food; slow service; wrong dishes provided; rude staff.
2 Quality assurance tries to prevent quality problems; quality control tries to identify and then correct quality problems.
3 Fewer materials wasted; less time spent fixing problems; less money spent sorting out customer returns; less supervision needed.

2.3.4

1 Training; retain experienced staff; recruit people who care about customers.
2 Making customers feel that they are a part of something, not an outsider.
3 Direct to the business; through word of mouth; on review sites.

2.4.1

1

	Company X	Company Y
Sales revenue	£25 million	£40 million
minus cost of sales	£10 million	£20 million
equals gross profit	£15 million	£20 million
minus fixed running costs	£10 million	£15 million
equals net profit	£5 million	£5 million
Gross profit margin	£15m / £25m × 100 = 60%	£20m / £40m × 100 = 50%
Net profit margin	£5m / £25m × 100 = 20%	£5m / £40m × 100 = 12.5%

2 Company X has higher gross and net profit margins, so is more profitable.

3 Lifetime profit = £200,000.
Average annual profit = £200,000 / 5 years = £40,000.
ARR = (£40,000 /£150,000) × 100 = 26.7%.

2.4.2

1 A line graph.
2 A pie chart.
3 The data may be unreliable; the manager may not interpret the data effectively.

2.5.1

1 Clear opportunities for promotion; easy to maintain standards throughout the firm; easy to supervise people closely.
2 Better local decision making; increased motivation for local staff.
3 Misunderstandings and rumours; inefficiency with a lack of sharing of ideas and solutions; low levels of motivation; lost profits.

2.5.2

1 Directors.
2 Job description; person specification.
3 Internal recruitment leaves a vacant post, left by the person appointed internally. If a firm is growing they simply need more people to come and work for them; moving staff from other areas of the business will not achieve this.

2.5.3

1 Formal training is planned; informal training happens as employees pick up tips from those around them.
2 As employees feel they are developing, they feel they have more to offer; staff who are trained will feel valued by their employer.
3 Training should reduce errors (which cost to fix) and speed up processes, meaning more can be done/produced in the same amount of time for the same cost (e.g. if an employee is paid £10 per hour and makes 5 units, the labour cost of each unit is £2. If the employee's training allows them to make 10 units per hour, the labour cost is only £1 per unit made).

2.5.4

1 Higher productivity; lower staff turnover, so lower recruitment cost; better quality levels; more ideas from staff.
2 Bonus; commission.
3 Job rotation expects employees to do a range of tasks, with the same level of responsibility; job enrichment offers tasks with increasing levels of challenge and responsibility to help employees grow.

Exam practice answers

Topic 1.1

1 1 mark for identification of a method, plus 2 further marks for explaining this method.
Methods include: branding, convenience, a USP, quality, design.
A lunch box manufacturer could produce a great design (1). Having a stylish design on the box is likely to make kids pester their parents to buy the box for them (1). As a result parents may be willing to pay more for the lunch box (1).

2 1 mark for identification of a risk, plus 2 further marks for explaining this risk.
Risks include: business failure, financial loss, loss of security.
An entrepreneur faces the risk of financial loss (1). If they invest money into starting the business, they will lose this money if the business goes bankrupt (2).

3 Up to 2 marks for linked points outlining the dynamic nature of business. Maximum of 1 mark if points are not linked.
Dynamic means changing (1), so because competitors constantly change what they do, the world of business is dynamic (1).
As technology changes regularly (1), consumer needs change as they demand new technologies, showing that business is dynamic (1).

4 Top level answers to 'discuss' questions will:
- demonstrate accurate knowledge and understanding of business concepts and issues throughout, including appropriate use of business terminology; and
- deconstruct business information and/or issues, finding detailed interconnected points with logical chains of reasoning.

Reasons why ideas may come about include: changing consumer needs; products becoming obsolete; changes in technology.
New ideas may emerge as products become obsolete (using terminology). If a business's main product is becoming obsolete, they will be forced to invest time and money into trying to generate new ideas if they want to sustain their sales (logical chain of reasoning and interconnected points made).

5 Top level answers to 'discuss' questions will:

- demonstrate accurate knowledge and understanding of business concepts and issues throughout, including appropriate use of business terminology; and
- deconstruct business information and/or issues, finding detailed interconnected points with logical chains of reasoning.

Rewards may include: business success; profit; independence.
A major reward may be profit (using terminology, showing knowledge). If a business is successful, they will make more money selling their products than it costs to run the business (showing understanding). The excess money is called profit and can be kept by the owner of the business, increasing their personal wealth (chain of logic built, interconnected points).

Topic 1.2

1 **b)** Focus group and **c)** One-to-one interviews.
2 **a)** Demographic.
3 **b)** Offer a good price and **c)** Develop innovative products.
4 **d)** Promotion.
5 1 mark for a benefit, plus 2 further marks for explaining it.
The market map helps to identify key features of competitors (1), helps the business to spot a gap in the market (1), so they can focus on features to hit that gap (1).
A market map can help a business make decisions about products (1) so that the features of the products are different from competitors (1), which makes it likely that they will be successful (1).
6 Up to 2 marks for linked points outlining a suitable reason.
Reasons could include:
- up-to-date information
- specific to the business's needs.
7 Up to 2 marks for linked points outlining a suitable reason.
Reasons could include:
- cheaper than primary market research (financially and in terms of time)
- likely to be based on a large, reliable sample.

Topic 1.3

1 a) Revenue = 1,800 x £80 = £144,000.
Costs = (1,800 x £30) + £40,000 = £94,000.
Profit = £144,000 − £94,000 = £50,000.

b) Fixed costs / (selling price − variable cost) = £40,000 / (£80 − £30) = 800.

c) Current sales − break-even point = 1,800 − 800 = 1,000 units.

2 A = £100; B = (£340), both in 000s.

3 Overdraft means you only pay for what you use; it looks like it would be paid off quickly as the cash flow forecast suggests the balance may be positive by month 7.

Buying new machinery would suit a longer term source of finance such as a bank loan. Interest rates on overdrafts tend to be higher than bank loans, so the bank loan would be a cheaper source of finance.

Detailed application of knowledge and understanding of factors affecting sources of finance and issues to the business context (using information from the cash flow forecast, recognising that machinery is a long-term asset) throughout.

Detailed interconnected points with logical chains of reasoning, explaining the benefits to the business of both sources.

A judgement on which source would be best, providing a clear justification based on a thorough evaluation of business information and issues relevant to the choice of source.

Topic 1.4

1 Has shareholders (1); shareholders have limited liability (1).

2 The business plan will help to raise finance (1), which Sophie needs as she is £17,500 short of the figure needed to start up (1).
The business plan will help Sophie think things through (1), which she may need as she does not seem to have experience of running her own salon (1).

3 Detailed application of knowledge and understanding of factors affecting location (proximity to customers, proximity to labour, proximity to competitors, proximity to materials and cost) and issues to the business context (using information from the table, recognising that a hair salon will not need to worry much about materials, but proximity to customers will be key: they must be present to have their hair done) throughout.
Detailed interconnected points with logical chains of reasoning, explaining the benefits to Sophie of both locations.

A judgement on which location would be best, providing a clear justification based on a thorough evaluation of business information and issues relevant to the choice of location.

Topic 1.5

1 Customers; suppliers; shareholders; employees.

2 Customers – good prices (1); decent quality (1).
Suppliers – paid on time (1); paid a fair price (1).
Shareholders – dividend payments (1).
Employees – a safe job (1); a decent wage (1).

3 With no need for a physical shop (1), there is no need to pay the high rents charged in high streets (1).

4 Promotion (1), so a business can provide information on its products via social media or show adverts (1).

5 c) Equality Act and **e)** Equal Pay Act.

6 Unemployment means fewer people have money to spend on luxuries (1) so sales of foreign holidays will fall (1).

7 A firm planning to expand may need to borrow money (1), so the interest payments will be lower (1).

8 Foreign consumers will get less of their currency for every pound, so UK products will seem more expensive (1), so sales are likely to fall (1).

Topic 2.1

1 c) Merger and **d)** Takeover.

2 a) Overdraft and **e)** Government grant.

3 If a business starts to make a loss (1) they may need to adjust what they are trying to achieve (1).

4 If demand for their product falls (1) they will not need to make as many and so can get rid of staff (1), which reduces costs (1).

5 Increased competition from imports (1) has forced them to cut prices or go out of business (1); many have been forced to move abroad (1) because they cannot pay UK costs and still charge a competitive price (1).

6 Trading blocs (1); tariffs (1).

7 The moral issues involved in running a business.

Topic 2.2

1 b) Promotion and **d)** People.

2 a) Production.

3 The aim of promotion in the introduction phase is to raise awareness (1); by the growth stage, promotion may start to focus on product differentiation (1).

4 The extent to which consumers see your product as being distinct from its rivals'.
5 **d)** Customer service.
6 Targeted advertising online; viral advertising via social media; e-newsletters (1 mark each, max 2).
7 Retailer.

Topic 2.3

1 Quality control means putting measures in place to check that the customer receives an acceptable level of quality.
2 Training (1) to explain the benefits of the new production process and to explain the change in product range (1).
3 The graph will help to manage stock, to ensure enough materials are in stock (1) and maintain a sensible buffer stock (1). The graph may also be used to know when to re-order new stock (1) (1 mark each, max 2).
4 Detailed application of knowledge and understanding of factors affecting procurement and issues to the business context (larger scale production – 5,000 units per week, need for dependable supplies) throughout.
Detailed interconnected points with logical chains of reasoning, explaining the benefits to Zebra Ltd of both suppliers: new one would offer lower costs and scope for more profit, but sticking with original would offer greater flexibility and an established relationship should mean trust exists.
A judgement on which supplier would be best, providing a clear justification based on a thorough evaluation of business information and issues relevant to the choice of supplier.
5 Detailed application of knowledge and understanding of batch and flow production and issues to the business context throughout, such as the desire to grow, the change to product range.
Detailed interconnected points with logical chains of reasoning, explaining the benefits to Zebra Ltd of both batch and flow production.
A judgement on whether flow production would generate more profit than batch production, providing a clear justification based on a thorough evaluation of business information and issues relevant to the choice of production method.

Topic 2.4

1 **a)** £200m − £120m = £80m.
  b) £80m / £200m × 100 = 40%.
  c) £20m / £200m × 100 = 10%.
2 Lifetime profit = £24m (3).
  Annual profit = £24m / 3 = £8m (1).
  ARR = £8m / £40m × 100 = 20% (3).
  Yes, the project's ARR of 20% is higher than the 12% target (2).
3 A line graph is best for trends.
4 A bar chart would allow bars for gross and net profit margin figures to be shown for each year.

Topic 2.5

1 Fringe benefits are rewards you get from work (1) other than pay (1), such as a company phone or car.
2 Fewer layers means easier communication (1), which makes it easier to stay abreast of changes in the market (1).
  Skilled, creative staff need less supervision (1) so fewer managers/supervisors are needed (1).
3 For top level marks, you need to show:
  ● detailed application of knowledge and understanding of internal and external recruitment and issues to the business context throughout, such as the existing staff being skilled and motivated, but with only 30 (29) staff to choose from the pool of applicants would be small
  ● detailed interconnected points with logical chains of reasoning, explaining the benefits to SoozeApps of both internal and external recruitment
  ● a judgement on whether internal or external recruitment would be best, providing a clear justification based on a thorough evaluation of business information and issues relevant to the choice of recruitment method.

Notes